Pasta&Casseroles

Pasta&Casseroles

Amazingly tasty...surprisingly simple!

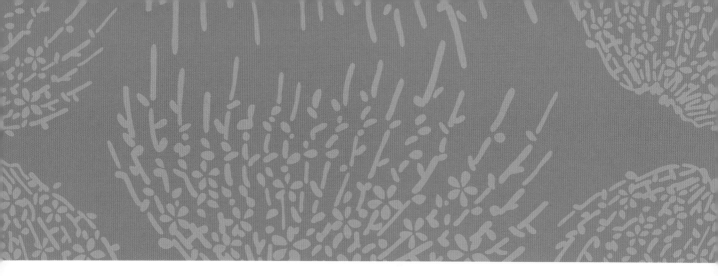

First published in 2010
LOVE FOOD is an imprint of Parragon Books Ltd

Parragon
Queen Street House
4 Queen Street
Bath BA1 1HE, UK

ISBN: 978-1-4075-5385-6

Printed in China

Cover design by Andrew Easton @ Ummagumma
Internal design by Ignition
Additional photography by Mike Cooper
Additional food styling by Lincoln Jefferson

Notes for the Reader

• This book uses imperial, metric, and US cup measurements. Follow the same units of measurement throughout; do not mix imperial and metric. All spoon measurements are level: teaspoons are assumed to be 5 ml, and tablespoons are assumed to be 15 ml. Unless otherwise stated, milk is assumed to be whole, eggs and individual vegetables are medium, and pepper is freshly ground black pepper.

• The times given are an approximate guide only. Preparation times differ according to the techniques used by different people and the cooking times may also vary from those given. Optional ingredients, variations, or serving suggestions have not been included in the calculations.

• Recipes using raw or very lightly cooked eggs should be avoided by infants, the elderly, pregnant women, convalescents, and anyone with a chronic illness. Pregnant and breast-feeding women are advised to avoid eating peanuts and peanut products. People with a nut allergy should be aware that some of the prepared ingredients used in the recipes in this book may contain nuts. Always check the package before use.

• Vegetarians should be aware that some of the prepared ingredients used in this book may contain animal product. Always check the package before use.

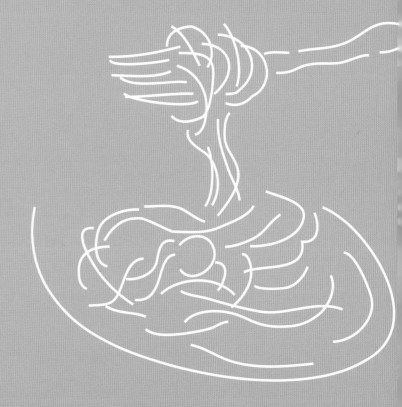

Pasta is arguably the most useful ingredient to be found in any kitchen. It goes with just about anything else you can think of—from vegetables and cheese to meat and fish. It's equally delicious served with simple, inexpensive sauces or extravagant and luxurious mixtures, and it can be added to soups or form the basis of filling baked dishes. It may be a main meal, an appetizer, or a delightfully different salad.

Pasta is very versatile so it's easy to find fabulous recipes for all occasions and every season of the year. Virtually everyone loves pasta and it's especially popular with children. High in complex carbohydrates, it provides a steady release of energy but contains hardly any fat. Depending on the type of wheat flour used in its manufacture, it can also be a good source of protein, as well as B vitamins, potassium, and iron. Moreover, it's economical, convenient, and the dried variety keeps well. Huge numbers of pasta dishes can be prepared and cooked within 30 minutes and many take only half that time.

There are hundreds of pasta shapes and new ones are being introduced all the time. There are no ironclad rules about which shape goes with a particular sauce, although there are some traditional partnerships, such as Spaghetti Bolognese and Macaroni & Cheese. However, there are some useful guidelines.

Long, thin pasta, such as spaghetti and linguine, is ideal for seafood sauces and light olive oil or fresh tomato dressings, but cannot really hold thick or chunky sauces. These are better served with pasta shapes that trap the sauce in hollows and ridges—penne (quills), fusilli (spirals), or conchiglie (shells), for example. Flat ribbons, such as tagliatelle, fettucine, and pappardelle, are perfect for rich or creamy sauces.

Baked dishes are often made with lasagne (flat sheets of pasta that can be layered with a variety of sauces) or cannelloni (tubes that can be filled and baked in a sauce). Smaller shapes, such as macaroni and rigatoni, are also often used in baking.

Very small pasta shapes, such as stellete (stars) and anellini (rings), are used in soups, and filled pasta, such as ravioli and tortellini, is also often served in broth.

Because there is such a huge variety of pasta shapes and sizes available, the cooking times in this book are only a guideline. Check the package directions for specific cooking times for the pasta you use.

MAKING FRESH PASTA

If you want to make filled pasta, such as tortellini, you will need to prepare the dough yourself. The same basic dough can also be used to make lasagna sheets and a variety of shapes, such as tagliatelle, pappardelle, and macaroni. You need no special equipment and the process is both easy and satisfying.

Basic Pasta Dough

Serves 3–4

Preparation time: 15 minutes, plus 30 minutes resting

1½ cups white bread flour, plus extra for dusting
pinch of salt
2 eggs, lightly beaten
1 tbsp olive oil

1 Sift together the flour and salt onto a work surface and make a well in the center with your fingers. Pour the eggs and oil into the well, then using the fingers of one hand, gradually incorporate the flour into the liquid.

2 Knead the dough on a lightly floured work surface until it is completely smooth. Wrap in plastic wrap and let rest for 30 minutes before rolling out or feeding through a pasta machine. Resting makes the dough more elastic.

FLAVORED PASTA

Basic pasta dough may be flavored and colored by the addition of other ingredients.

Tomato pasta: Add 2 tbsp tomato paste to the well in the flour and use only 1½ eggs instead of 2.

Spinach pasta: Blanch 8 oz/225 g spinach in boiling water for 1 minute, then drain and squeeze out as much liquid as possible. Alternatively, use 5½ oz/150 g thawed frozen spinach. This does not need blanching, but as much liquid as possible should be squeezed out. Finely chop the spinach and mix with the flour before making a well and adding the eggs and oil.

Herb pasta: Add 3 tbsp finely chopped fresh herbs to the flour before making a well and adding the eggs and oil.

Saffron pasta: Soak an envelope of powdered saffron in 2 tbsp hot water for 15 minutes. Use 1½ eggs and whisk the saffron water into them.

Whole wheat pasta: Use 1 cup plus 3 tbsp whole wheat flour and 3 tbsp white bread flour.

ROLLING OUT PASTA DOUGH

When the fresh dough has rested, it may be rolled out by hand or with a pasta machine. Larger quantities of dough should be halved or cut into thirds before rolling out. Keep covered until you are ready to work on them.

To roll out by hand, lightly dust a work surface with all-purpose flour, then roll out the pasta dough with a lightly floured rolling pin, always rolling away from you and turning the dough a quarter turn each time. Keep rolling to make a rectangle ¹⁄₁₆–⅛ inch/ 2–3 mm thick. The dough can then be cut into ribbons, stamped out with a cookie cutter, or cut into squares to make ravioli.

A pasta machine makes rolling out the dough easier and quicker and ensures that it is even. There are a number of models available, the most useful being a hand-cranked machine with attachable cutters. An electric machine is even easier to use but somewhat extravagant.

Cut the dough into manageable-size pieces— 1 quantity Basic Pasta Dough should be cut into 4 pieces, for example. Flatten a piece with your hand and wrap the others in plastic wrap until required. Fold the flat piece into thirds and feed it through the pasta machine on its widest setting. Repeat the folding and rolling 3 or 4 more times on this setting, then close the rollers by one notch. Continue feeding the dough through the rollers, without folding into thirds, gradually reducing the setting until you reach the narrowest. If you want to make ribbons, cut the dough into 12-inch/30-cm strips and feed through the appropriate cutter.

CUTTING AND SHAPING FRESH PASTA

Pasta machines usually have a wide cutter for tagliatelle and a narrower one for tagliarini. Other pasta shapes can be cut by hand, as can hand-rolled pasta dough.

To make pappardelle, use a serrated pasta wheel to cut 1-inch/2.5-cm-wide ribbons from the rolled-out dough. To make tagliatelle or tagliarini, roll up a strip of dough like a jelly roll and then cut into ¼-inch/ 5-mm slices (tagliatelle) or ⅛-inch/3-mm slices (tagliarini) with a sharp knife. To make macaroni, cut the pasta dough into 1-inch/2.5-cm squares with a sharp knife, then roll them corner to corner around a chopstick to form tubes. Slide off and let dry slightly.

Italians use the word *ravioli* as an all-purpose term for filled pasta and it can, therefore, be a variety of shapes.

Soups & Salads

SERVES 4

2 tbsp olive oil
2 garlic cloves, chopped
2 red onions, chopped
2¾ oz/75 g prosciutto, sliced
1 red bell pepper, seeded and chopped
1 orange bell pepper, seeded and chopped

14 oz/400 g canned chopped tomatoes
4 cups vegetable stock
1 celery stalk, trimmed and sliced
14 oz/400 g canned cranberry beans, drained
1 cup shredded green leafy cabbage

½ cup thawed frozen peas
1 tbsp chopped fresh parsley
2¾ oz/75 g dried vermicelli
salt and pepper
freshly grated Parmesan cheese, to serve

Minestrone

Heat the oil in a large pan. Add the garlic, onions, and prosciutto and cook over medium heat, stirring, for 3 minutes, until slightly softened. Add the red and orange bell peppers and the chopped tomatoes and cook for an additional 2 minutes, stirring. Stir in the stock, then add the celery, cranberry beans, cabbage, peas, and parsley. Season to taste with salt and pepper. Bring to a boil, then lower the heat and simmer for 30 minutes.

Add the vermicelli to the pan. Cook for another 10–12 minutes, or according to the instructions on the package. Remove from the heat and ladle into serving bowls. Sprinkle with freshly grated Parmesan and serve immediately.

SERVES 4

2 tomatoes, chopped
1 garlic clove, chopped
¼ onion, chopped
1 tbsp vegetable oil
4¾ cups chicken or
    vegetable stock
4 oz/115 g vermicelli,
    broken into short
    lengths

¼–½ fresh red chile,
    seeded and finely
    sliced
3½ cups shredded baby
    kale or spinach, tough
    stems removed
3 tbsp chopped cilantro
½ cup diced feta cheese

4 tbsp sour cream
salt and pepper
finely diced red onion,
    to garnish

Mexican vermicelli Soup

Put the tomatoes, garlic, and onion in a blender and process until a smooth paste has formed. Heat a small skillet, add the oil, and cook the paste over medium heat for about 5 minutes, until slightly reduced.

Bring the stock to a boil in a large saucepan. Add the vermicelli and cook for 5 minutes, then add the chile, kale, and the reduced paste. Season to taste with salt and pepper. Cover and simmer over medium–low heat for 6–8 minutes, until the vermicelli is tender. Stir in 2 tablespoons of the cilantro.

Put the cheese in the bottom of individual bowls, then ladle the soup over the top. Add a tablespoon of sour cream to each bowl, and sprinkle with red onion and the remaining cilantro. Serve immediately.

SERVES 6

10½ oz/300 g canned cannellini beans, drained and rinsed
10½ oz/300 g canned cranberry beans, drained and rinsed

about 2½ cups chicken or vegetable stock
4 oz/115 g dried conchigliette (small pasta shells)
4–5 tbsp olive oil

2 garlic cloves, very finely chopped
3 tbsp chopped fresh flat-leaf parsley
salt and pepper

Tuscan Bean Soup

Place half the cannellini and half the cranberry beans in a food processor with half the stock and process until smooth. Pour into a large, heavy-bottom pan and add the remaining beans. Stir in enough of the remaining stock to achieve the consistency you like, then bring to a boil.

Add the pasta and return to a boil, then reduce the heat and cook for 15 minutes, or until just tender.

Meanwhile, heat 3 tablespoons of the oil in a small skillet. Add the garlic and cook, stirring constantly, for 2–3 minutes, or until golden. Stir the garlic into the soup with the parsley.

Season to taste with salt and pepper and ladle into warmed soup bowls. Drizzle with the remaining olive oil to taste and serve immediately.

SERVES 4

2 tbsp olive oil
3 strips smoked bacon,
    chopped
2 tbsp butter
4 starchy potatoes,
    about 1 lb/450 g, finely
    chopped

3 onions, about 1 lb/
    450 g, finely chopped
2½ cups chicken stock
2½ cups milk
3½ oz/100 g dried
    conchigliette
    (small pasta shells)

⅔ cup heavy cream
2 tbsp chopped fresh
    parsley
2 tbsp green pesto
salt and pepper
freshly grated Parmesan
    cheese, to serve

Potato & Pesto Soup

Heat the oil in a large saucepan and cook the bacon over medium heat for
4 minutes. Add the butter, potatoes, and onions, and cook for 12 minutes, stirring
constantly.

Add the stock and milk to the pan, bring to a boil, and simmer for 5 minutes. Add
the conchigliette and simmer for an additional 3–5 minutes.

Blend in the cream and simmer for 5 minutes. Add the parsley and pesto and
season to taste with salt and pepper. Sprinkle with freshly grated Parmesan cheese
and serve immediately.

SERVES 4

4 strips lean bacon, cut into small squares
1 onion, chopped
2 garlic cloves, crushed
2 celery stalks, chopped

1¾ oz/50 g dried farfallini (small pasta bows)
14 oz/400 g canned brown lentils, drained

5 cups vegetable stock
2 tbsp chopped fresh mint, plus extra sprigs to garnish

Brown Lentil & Pasta Soup

Place the bacon in a large skillet together with the onion, garlic, and celery. Cook for 4–5 minutes, stirring, until the onion is tender and the bacon is just beginning to brown.

Add the pasta to the skillet and cook, stirring, for 1 minute to coat the pasta in the fat.

Add the lentils and stock, and bring to a boil. Reduce the heat and simmer for 12–15 minutes, or until the pasta is tender but still firm to the bite.

Remove the skillet from the heat and stir in the chopped fresh mint. Transfer the soup to warmed soup bowls, garnish with fresh mint sprigs, and serve immediately.

SERVES 6

1 quantity Basic Pasta
   Dough (see p. 6)
egg white, for brushing
flour, for dusting
8 cups chicken stock
2 tbsp finely chopped
   fresh tarragon leaves

filling
1⅓ cups coarsely
   chopped cooked
   chicken
½ tsp grated lemon rind
2 tbsp chopped mixed
   fresh tarragon, chives,
   and parsley

4 tbsp heavy cream
freshly grated Parmesan,
   to serve
salt and pepper

Chicken Ravioli in Tarragon Broth

To make the filling, put the chicken, lemon rind, and mixed herbs in a food processor and season to taste with salt and pepper. Chop finely by pulsing; do not overprocess. Scrape into a bowl and stir in the cream. Taste and adjust the seasoning, if necessary.

Divide the pasta dough in half. Cover one half and roll the other half on a floured surface as thinly as possible, less than 1/16 inch/1.5 mm. Cut out rectangles about 4 x 2 inches/10 x 5 cm.

Place rounded teaspoons of filling on one half of the dough pieces. Brush around the edges with egg white and fold in half. Press the edges gently but firmly to seal. Arrange the ravioli in one layer on a baking sheet, dusted generously with flour. Repeat with the remaining dough. Let the ravioli dry in a cool place for about 15 minutes, or chill for 1–2 hours.

Bring a large quantity of water to a boil. Drop in half the ravioli and cook for 12–15 minutes, until just tender. Drain on a clean dish towel while cooking the remainder.

Meanwhile, put the stock and tarragon in a large saucepan. Bring to a boil and reduce the heat to bubble very gently. Cover and simmer for about 15 minutes to steep. Add the cooked ravioli to the stock and simmer for about 5 minutes, until reheated. Ladle into warmed soup bowls to serve, sprinkled with grated Parmesan.

SERVES 4

1 lb/450 g skinless,
boneless chicken
breast, cut into thin
strips
5 cups chicken stock

²/₃ cup heavy cream
4 oz/115 g dried
vermicelli
1 tbsp cornstarch
3 tbsp milk

6 oz/175 g canned corn
kernels, drained
salt and pepper

Italian Chicken Soup

Place the chicken in a large pan and pour in the chicken stock and cream. Bring to a boil, then reduce the heat and simmer for 20 minutes.

Meanwhile, bring a large, heavy-bottom pan of lightly salted water to a boil. Add the pasta, return to a boil, and cook for 10–12 minutes, or until just tender but still firm to the bite. Drain the pasta well and keep warm.

Season the saucepan of chicken to taste with salt and pepper. Mix the cornstarch and milk together until a smooth paste forms, then stir it into the soup. Add the corn and pasta and heat through. Ladle the soup into warmed soup bowls and serve immediately.

SERVES 6

1 tbsp olive oil
1 lb 2 oz/500 g fresh lean
    ground beef
2 onions, finely chopped
2 garlic cloves, finely
    chopped
2 tbsp all-purpose flour
1 cup water

14 oz/400 g canned
    chopped tomatoes
1 carrot, finely chopped
1 large red bell pepper,
    roasted, peeled,
    seeded, and chopped
1 tsp Hungarian paprika
¼ tsp caraway seeds

pinch of dried oregano
4 cups beef stock
2 oz/55 g tagliatelle,
    broken into small
    pieces
salt and pepper
sour cream and sprigs of
    fresh cilantro, to garnish

Beef Goulash Soup

Heat the oil in a large, wide saucepan over medium–high heat. Add the beef and season to taste with salt and pepper. Cook until lightly browned.

Reduce the heat and add the onions and garlic. Cook for about 3 minutes, stirring frequently, until the onions are softened. Stir in the flour and continue cooking for 1 minute.

Gradually stir in the water and combine well, scraping the bottom of the pan to mix in the flour. Stir in the tomatoes, carrot, bell pepper, paprika, caraway seeds, oregano, and stock.

Bring just to a boil. Reduce the heat, cover, and simmer gently for about 40 minutes, stirring occasionally, until all the vegetables are tender.

Add the tagliatelle to the soup and simmer for an additional 20 minutes, or until the tagliatelle is cooked.

Taste the soup and adjust the seasoning, if necessary. Ladle into warmed bowls and top each with a tablespoonful of sour cream. Garnish with cilantro and serve.

SERVES 4

⅓ cup dried peas, soaked for 2 hours and drained
2 lb/900 g boned shoulder of veal, diced
5 cups beef stock
2½ cups water

⅓ cup pearl barley, washed
1 large carrot, diced
1 small turnip (about 6 oz/175 g), diced
1 large leek, thinly sliced
1 red onion, finely chopped

3½ oz/100 g chopped tomatoes
1 fresh basil sprig
3 oz/85 g dried vermicelli
salt and white pepper

Tuscan Veal Broth

Put the peas, veal, stock, and water into a large pan and bring to a boil over low heat. Using a slotted spoon, skim off any foam that rises to the surface.

When all of the foam has been removed, add the pearl barley and a pinch of salt to the mixture. Simmer gently over low heat for 25 minutes.

Add the carrot, turnip, leek, onion, tomatoes, and basil to the pan, and season to taste with salt and pepper. Simmer for about 2 hours, skimming the surface from time to time to remove any foam. Remove the pan from the heat and set aside for 2 hours.

Set the pan over medium heat and bring to a boil. Add the vermicelli and cook for 8–10 minutes, then remove and discard the basil. Ladle into soup bowls and serve immediately.

SERVES 6

2 tbsp olive oil
2 onions, sliced
1 garlic clove, finely
  chopped
4 cups fish stock or water
14 oz/400 g canned
  chopped tomatoes

¼ tsp Herbes de Provence
¼ tsp saffron threads
4 oz/115 g dried
  macaroni
18 mussels, scrubbed
  and debearded

1 lb/450 g monkfish fillet,
  cut into chunks
8 oz/225 g shrimp,
  shelled and deveined,
  tails left on
salt and pepper

Fish Soup with Macaroni

Heat the olive oil in a large, heavy-bottom pan. Add the onions and garlic and cook over low heat, stirring occasionally, for 5 minutes, or until the onions have softened.

Add the stock with the tomatoes and their can juices, herbs, saffron, and pasta, and season to taste with salt and pepper. Bring to a boil, then cover and simmer for 15 minutes.

Discard any mussels with broken shells or any that refuse to close when tapped. Add the mussels, monkfish, and shrimp to the pan. Re-cover and simmer for an additional 5–10 minutes, until the mussels have opened, the shrimp have changed color, and the fish is opaque and flakes easily. Discard any mussels that remain closed. Ladle the soup into warmed bowls and serve.

SERVES 4

1 lb 10 oz/750 g mussels, scrubbed and debearded
2 tbsp olive oil
½ cup butter
2 oz/55 g rindless lean bacon, chopped

1 onion, chopped
2 garlic cloves, finely chopped
⅓ cup all-purpose flour
3 potatoes, thinly sliced
4 oz/115 g dried farfalle (pasta bows)

1¼ cups heavy cream
1 tbsp lemon juice
2 egg yolks
salt and pepper
2 tbsp finely chopped fresh parsley, to garnish

Mussel & Pasta Soup

Discard any mussels with broken shells or any that refuse to close when tapped. Bring a large, heavy-bottom pan of water to a boil. Add the mussels and olive oil and season to taste with pepper. Cover tightly and cook over high heat for 5 minutes, or until the mussels have opened. Remove the mussels with a slotted spoon, discarding any that remain closed. Strain the cooking liquid and set aside 5 cups.

Melt the butter in a clean pan. Add the bacon, onion, and garlic, and cook over low heat, stirring occasionally, for 5 minutes. Stir in the flour and cook, stirring, for 1 minute. Gradually stir in all but 2 tablespoons of the reserved cooking liquid and bring to a boil, stirring constantly. Add the potato slices and simmer for 5 minutes. Add the pasta and simmer for an additional 10 minutes.

Stir in the cream and lemon juice and season to taste with salt and pepper. Add the mussels. Mix the egg yolks and the remaining mussel cooking liquid together, then stir the mixture into the soup and cook for 4 minutes, until thickened.

Ladle the soup into warmed soup bowls, garnish with chopped parsley, and serve immediately.

SERVES 6

1 lb 2 oz/500 g shelled scallops
1½ cups milk
6¼ cups basic vegetable stock
1¾ cups frozen young peas

6 oz/175 g taglialini
5 tbsp butter
2 scallions, finely chopped
¾ cup dry white wine

3 slices of prosciutto, cut into thin strips
salt and pepper
chopped fresh parsley, to garnish

Quick Sea Scallop Soup with Pasta

Slice the scallops in half horizontally and season with salt and pepper.

Pour the milk and stock into a saucepan, add a pinch of salt, and bring to a boil. Add the peas and taglialini, bring back to a boil and cook for 8–10 minutes, until the taglialini is tender but still firm to the bite.

Meanwhile, melt the butter in a skillet. Add the scallions and cook over low heat, stirring occasionally, for 3 minutes. Add the scallops and cook for 45 seconds on each side. Pour in the wine, add the prosciutto, and cook for 2–3 minutes.

Stir the scallop mixture into the soup, taste, and adjust the seasoning, if necessary. Garnish with parsley and serve immediately.

SERVES 4

1 lb/450 g round or sirloin steak in a single piece
8 oz/225 g dried fusilli (pasta spirals)
4 tbsp olive oil
2 tbsp lime juice

2 tbsp Thai fish sauce
2 tsp honey
4 scallions, sliced
1 cucumber, peeled and cut into 1-inch/2.5-cm chunks

3 tomatoes, cut into wedges
1 tbsp finely chopped fresh mint
salt and pepper

Rare Roast Beef Pasta Salad

Season the steak with salt and pepper. Broil or pan-fry it for 4 minutes on each side. Let rest for 5 minutes, then slice thinly across the grain.

Meanwhile, bring a large pan of lightly salted water to a boil. Add the pasta, bring back to a boil, and cook for 8–10 minutes, or until tender but still firm to the bite. Drain the pasta, refresh in cold water, and drain again thoroughly. Toss the fusilli in the olive oil and set aside until required.

Combine the lime juice, fish sauce, and honey in a small pan and cook over medium heat for 2 minutes.

Add the scallions, cucumber, tomatoes, and mint to the pan, then add the steak and mix well. Season to taste with salt.

Transfer the fusilli to a large, warm serving dish and top with the steak and salad mixture. Serve just warm or let cool completely.

SERVES 4-6

4 oz/115 g egg pappardelle, broken into 3-inch/7.5-cm lengths
coarsely grated zest of 1 lemon

2 tbsp extra virgin olive oil
4 carrots
2 zucchini
1 cup thinly sliced cooked chicken
1/3 cup walnut halves

5 tbsp snipped fresh chives
2 tsp white wine vinegar
3 tbsp walnut oil
1/2 tsp salt
1/4 tsp pepper

Chicken Pasta Salad with Walnuts

Bring a pan of lightly salted water to a boil over medium heat. Add the pasta and cook for 8–10 minutes, or until tender but still firm to the bite. Drain the pasta thoroughly and turn into a serving bowl. Toss with the lemon zest, 1 tablespoon of the olive oil, and season to taste with salt and pepper.

Meanwhile, trim and peel the carrots. Slice lengthwise into thin strips, using a mandoline or very sharp knife. Trim the zucchini, and remove a wide band of peel on opposite sides. Slice lengthwise into thin strips, so that there is a narrow strip of green peel on each side. Put the carrots in a steamer basket set over boiling water. Steam for 3 minutes, then add the zucchini. Steam for 2 minutes more until only just tender.

Add the vegetables, chicken, walnuts, and chives to the pasta, tossing gently to mix. Whisk the vinegar with the salt and pepper. Whisk in the walnut oil and the remaining tablespoon of olive oil. Pour over the salad and toss again carefully. Let stand for 30 minutes to let the flavor develop. Serve at room temperature.

SERVES 4

4½ oz/125 g dried conchiglie (pasta shells)
2 tbsp olive oil
1 medium onion, chopped
2 garlic cloves, very finely chopped

1 small yellow bell pepper, seeded and cut into very thin sticks
6 oz/175 g spicy pork sausage, such as chorizo, pepperoni, or salami, skinned and sliced

2 tbsp red wine
1 tbsp red wine vinegar
4 oz/125 g mixed salad greens
salt

Spicy Sausage Salad

Bring a large pan of lightly salted water to a boil over medium heat. Add the pasta and cook for 8–10 minutes, or until tender but still firm to the bite. Drain the pasta and set aside.

Heat the oil in a pan over medium heat. Add the onion and cook until translucent, then stir in the garlic, bell pepper, and sausage, and cook for 3–4 minutes, stirring once or twice.

Add the wine, wine vinegar, and reserved pasta to the pan, stir, and bring the mixture just to a boil over medium heat.

Arrange the salad greens on serving plates, spoon the warm sausage-and-pasta mixture on top, and serve immediately.

SERVES 6

8 oz/225 g dried fusilli
  (pasta spirals)
4 tomatoes, peeled
½ cup black olives
2 tbsp sun-dried
  tomatoes in oil, drained
2 tbsp pine nuts,
  dry-roasted

2 tbsp freshly grated
  Parmesan cheese
salt
1 fresh basil sprig,
  to garnish

pesto vinaigrette
4 tbsp chopped fresh
  basil

1 garlic clove, very finely
  chopped
2 tbsp freshly grated
  Parmesan cheese
4 tbsp olive oil
2 tbsp lemon juice
pepper

Pasta Salad with Pesto Vinaigrette

Bring a large pan of lightly salted water to a boil over medium heat. Add the pasta and cook for 8–10 minutes, or until tender but still firm to the bite. Drain the pasta thoroughly, rinse well in hot water, then drain again. Set aside.

To make the pesto vinaigrette, whisk the basil, garlic, Parmesan cheese, oil, and lemon juice together in a small bowl until well blended. Season to taste with pepper.

Put the pasta into a bowl, pour the pesto vinaigrette over it, and toss thoroughly.

Cut the tomatoes into wedges. Halve and pit the olives and slice the sun-dried tomatoes. Add the tomatoes, olives, and sun-dried tomatoes to the pasta and toss well.

Transfer the pasta to a salad bowl and sprinkle the pine nuts and Parmesan cheese over the top. Garnish with a basil sprig and serve warm.

SERVES 4-6

8 oz/225 g pasta shapes, such as farfalle or fusilli
5 scallions, some green included, sliced
2 cups shelled baby fava beans (frozen or fresh)

3½ oz/100 g thinly sliced chorizo
6 tbsp extra virgin olive oil
2 shallots, finely chopped
2 tbsp red wine vinegar
2 tbsp chopped fresh thyme or marjoram

squeeze of lemon juice
¼ tsp dried chile flakes
salt and pepper

Fava Bean, Chorizo & Pasta Salad

Bring a pan of lightly salted water to a boil over medium heat. Add the pasta and cook for 8–10 minutes, or until tender but still firm to the bite. Drain the pasta and transfer to a serving dish. Add the scallions, tossing to mix.

Meanwhile, put the fava beans in a pan of boiling water. Bring back to a boil and cook for 4 minutes if frozen, 3 minutes if fresh, or until just tender. Drain under cold running water and pat dry with paper towels. Peel away the outer skins if they are tough. Mix with the pasta and scallions.

Cut the chorizo slices into quarters. Heat a large skillet over medium–high heat. Cook the chorizo in a single layer for 3–4 minutes until beginning to blacken slightly. Add to the pasta mixture and toss well.

Reduce the heat to medium–low and warm the olive oil. Add the shallots and gently cook for 2 minutes, until softened. Swirl in the vinegar and cook for a few extra seconds. Turn the contents of the pan over the pasta mixture and toss to coat.

Stir in the thyme or marjoram, lemon juice, and chile flakes, and season to taste with salt and pepper. Toss thoroughly to mix, then let stand at room temperature for 30 minutes to let the flavor develop. Toss again and add more seasoning, if necessary. Serve at room temperature.

SERVES 4

9 oz/250 g dried penne (pasta quills)
1 head of radicchio, torn into pieces
1 head of lettuce, torn into pieces
7 tbsp chopped walnuts

2 ripe pears, cored and diced
½ cup arugula
2 tbsp lemon juice
5 tbsp olive oil
1 garlic clove, chopped
3 tbsp white wine vinegar

4 tomatoes, cut into wedges
1 small onion, sliced
1 large carrot, grated
9 oz/250 g goat cheese, diced
salt

Penne with Goat Cheese, Pears & Walnuts

Bring a large pan of lightly salted water to a boil over medium heat. Add the pasta and cook for 8–10 minutes, or until tender but still firm to the bite. Drain the pasta thoroughly and refresh in cold water, then drain again and set aside to cool.

Put the radicchio and iceberg lettuce into a large salad bowl and mix together well. Top with the cooled pasta, chopped walnuts, pears, and arugula.

Mix the lemon juice, oil, garlic, and vinegar together in a pitcher. Pour the mixture over the salad ingredients and toss to coat the salad greens well.

Add the tomato wedges, onion slices, grated carrot, and diced goat cheese and toss together with 2 forks, until well mixed. Let the salad chill in the refrigerator for about 1 hour before serving.

SERVES 4

8 oz/225 g dried farfalle (pasta bows)
6 pieces of sun-dried tomato in oil, drained and chopped
4 scallions, chopped

1¼ cups shredded arugula
½ cucumber, seeded and diced
2 tbsp freshly grated Parmesan cheese
salt and pepper

dressing
4 tbsp olive oil
1 tbsp white wine vinegar
½ tsp superfine sugar
1 tsp Dijon mustard
4 fresh basil leaves, finely shredded
salt and pepper

Warm Pasta Salad

To make the dressing, whisk the olive oil, vinegar, sugar, and mustard together in a bowl or pitcher. Season to taste with salt and pepper and stir in the basil.

Bring a large, heavy-bottom pan of lightly salted water to a boil. Add the pasta, return to a boil, and cook for 8–10 minutes, or until tender but still firm to the bite. Drain the pasta and transfer to a salad bowl. Add the dressing and toss well.

Add the tomatoes, scallions, arugula, and cucumber, season to taste with salt and pepper, and toss. Divide among individual plates, sprinkle with the Parmesan cheese, and serve warm.

SERVES 4

9 oz/250 g dried orecchiette
1 head of radicchio, torn into pieces
1 oak leaf lettuce, torn into pieces
2 pears
1 tbsp lemon juice

9 oz/250 g bleu cheese, diced
scant ½ cup chopped walnuts
4 tomatoes, quartered
1 red onion, sliced
1 carrot, grated

8 fresh basil leaves
2 cups corn salad

dressing
4 tbsp olive oil
2 tbsp lemon juice
salt and pepper

Orecchiette Salad with Pears + Bleu Cheese

Bring a large, heavy-bottom pan of lightly salted water to a boil. Add the pasta, return to a boil, and cook for 8–10 minutes, or until tender but still firm to the bite. Drain the pasta, refresh in a bowl of cold water, and drain again.

Place the radicchio and oak leaf lettuce leaves in a large bowl. Halve the pears, remove the cores, and dice the flesh. Toss the diced pear with 1 tablespoon of lemon juice in a small bowl to prevent discoloration. Top the salad with the bleu cheese, walnuts, pears, pasta, tomatoes, onion slices, and grated carrot. Add the basil and corn salad.

For the dressing, mix the lemon juice and the olive oil together in a measuring cup, then season to taste with salt and pepper. Pour the dressing over the salad, toss, and serve.

SERVES 4

2 large heads of lettuce
9 oz/250 g dried penne
  (pasta quills)
8 red apples

juice of 4 lemons
1 bunch of celery, sliced
¾ cup shelled, halved
  walnuts

1 cup fresh garlic
  mayonnaise
salt

Penne & Apple Salad

Wash and drain the lettuce leaves, then pat them dry with paper towels. Transfer them to the refrigerator for 1 hour, until crisp.

Meanwhile, bring a large pan of lightly salted water to a boil. Add the pasta, bring back to a boil, and cook for 8–10 minutes, or until tender but still firm to the bite. Drain the pasta and refresh under cold running water. Drain again thoroughly and set aside.

Core and dice the apples, then place them in a small bowl and sprinkle with the lemon juice. Mix together the pasta, celery, apples, and walnut halves and toss the mixture in the garlic mayonnaise. Add more mayonnaise, to taste.

Line a salad bowl with the lettuce leaves and spoon the pasta salad into the lined bowl. Refrigerate until ready to serve.

SERVES 6

8 oz/225 g dried green fusilli (pasta spirals)
5 tbsp extra virgin olive oil
1 lb/450 g cooked shrimp
1 cantaloupe melon
1 honeydew melon

1 tbsp red wine vinegar
1 tsp Dijon mustard
pinch of superfine sugar
1 tbsp chopped fresh flat-leaf parsley

1 tbsp chopped fresh basil, plus extra sprigs to garnish
1 oak leaf lettuce, shredded
salt and pepper

Pasta Salad with Melon & Shrimp

Bring a large pan of lightly salted water to a boil. Add the pasta, bring back to a boil, and cook for 8–10 minutes, until tender but still firm to the bite. Drain the pasta, toss with 1 tablespoon of the olive oil, and let cool.

Meanwhile, peel and devein the shrimp, then place them in a large bowl. Halve both the melons and scoop out the seeds with a spoon. Using a melon baller or teaspoon, scoop out balls of the flesh and add them to the shrimp.

Whisk together the remaining olive oil, the vinegar, mustard, sugar, parsley, and basil in a small bowl. Season to taste with salt and pepper. Add the cooled pasta to the shrimp-and-melon mixture and toss lightly to mix, then pour in the dressing and toss again. Cover with plastic wrap and chill in the refrigerator for 30 minutes.

Make a bed of shredded lettuce on individual plates. Spoon the pasta salad on top, garnish with basil leaves, and serve.

SERVES 4

1 cup 2-inch/5-cm
  pieces of green beans
8 oz/225 g dried fusilli
  (pasta spirals)
½ cup olive oil
2 tuna steaks, about
  12 oz/350 g each

6 cherry tomatoes,
  halved
⅓ cup pitted and halved
  black olives
6 canned anchovies,
  drained and chopped

3 tbsp chopped fresh
  flat-leaf parsley
2 tbsp lemon juice
8–10 radicchio leaves
salt and pepper

Pasta Niçoise

Bring a large, heavy-bottom pan of lightly salted water to a boil. Add the green beans, reduce the heat, and cook for 5–6 minutes. Remove with a slotted spoon and refresh in a bowl of cold water. Drain well. Add the pasta to the same pan, return to a boil, and cook for 8–10 minutes, or until the pasta is tender but still firm to the bite.

Meanwhile, brush a ridged grill pan with some of the olive oil and heat until smoking. Season the tuna to taste with salt and pepper and brush both sides with some of the remaining olive oil. Cook over medium heat for 2 minutes on each side, or until cooked to your liking, then remove from the grill pan and reserve.

Drain the pasta well and turn it into a bowl. Add the beans, tomatoes, olives, anchovies, parsley, lemon juice, and remaining olive oil and season to taste with salt and pepper. Toss well and let cool. Remove and discard any skin from the tuna and break into chunks.

Gently mix the tuna into the pasta salad. Line a large salad bowl with the radicchio leaves, spoon in the salad, and serve.

SERVES 2

3½ oz/100 g small whole wheat pasta
2 tbsp olive oil
1 tbsp mayonnaise
1 tbsp plain yogurt
2 tbsp pesto

7 oz/200 g canned tuna in spring water, drained and flaked
7 oz/200 g canned no-added-sugar corn kernels, drained

2 tomatoes, peeled, seeded, and chopped
½ green bell pepper, seeded and chopped
½ avocado, pitted, peeled, and chopped
salt and pepper

Tuna & Pasta Salad

Bring a large pan of lightly salted water to a boil. Add the pasta, bring back to a boil, and cook for 8–10 minutes, or until tender but still firm to the bite. Drain, return to the pan, and add half the oil. Toss well to coat, then cover and let cool.

Whisk the mayonnaise, yogurt, and pesto together in a pitcher, adding a little oil if needed to achieve the desired consistency. Season to taste with salt and pepper.

Mix the cooled pasta with the tuna, corn, tomatoes, bell pepper, and avocado, add the dressing, and toss well to coat.

SERVES 4

1 lb/450 g prepared squid, cut into strips
1 lb 10 oz/750 g cooked mussels
1 lb/450 g cooked cockles in brine
⅔ cup white wine
1¼ cups olive oil
8 oz/225 g dried campanelle or other small pasta shapes
juice of 1 lemon
1 bunch chives, snipped
1 bunch fresh parsley, finely chopped
salt and pepper
mixed salad leaves, to garnish
4 large tomatoes, to garnish

Neapolitan Seafood Salad

Put all of the seafood into a large bowl, pour in the wine and half of the olive oil, and set aside for 6 hours.

Put the seafood mixture into a saucepan and simmer over low heat for 10 minutes. Set aside to cool.

Bring a large pan of lightly salted water to a boil over medium heat. Add the pasta and 1 tbsp of the remaining olive oil and cook for 8–10 minutes, or until tender but still firm to the bite. Drain the pasta thoroughly and refresh in cold water.

Strain off about half of the cooking liquid from the seafood and discard the rest. Mix in the lemon juice, chives, parsley, and the remaining olive oil. Season to taste with salt and pepper. Drain the pasta and add to the seafood.

Shred the salad greens and divide them among individual plates. Cut the tomatoes into quarters. Divide the seafood salad among the plates, garnish with the tomatoes, and serve.

Meat & Poultry

SERVES 4

1 tbsp olive oil
1 onion, finely chopped
2 garlic cloves, chopped
1 carrot, chopped
1 celery stalk, chopped
1¾ oz/50 g pancetta or
    bacon, diced

12 oz/350 g lean ground
    beef
14 oz/400 g canned
    chopped tomatoes
2 tsp dried oregano
½ cup red wine
2 tbsp tomato paste

12 oz/350 g dried
    spaghetti
salt and pepper
chopped fresh flat-leaf
    parsley, to garnish

Spaghetti Bolognese

Heat the oil in a large skillet. Add the onion and cook for 3 minutes. Add the garlic, carrot, celery, and pancetta and cook for 3–4 minutes, or until just beginning to brown.

Add the beef and cook over high heat for an additional 3 minutes, or until the meat has browned. Stir in the tomatoes, oregano, and red wine and bring to a boil. Reduce the heat and simmer for about 45 minutes.

Stir in the tomato paste and season to taste with salt and pepper.

Cook the spaghetti in a pan of lightly salted boiling water for 8–10 minutes, or until tender but still firm to the bite. Drain the pasta thoroughly.

Transfer the spaghetti to individual warmed dishes and pour the bolognese sauce on top. Toss to mix well, garnish with parsley, and serve immediately.

SERVES 6

¾ cup olive oil
4 tbsp butter
½ cup diced bacon or pancetta
1 onion, finely chopped
1 celery stalk, finely chopped
1 carrot, finely chopped

12 oz/350 g beef pot roast, in a single piece
5 tbsp red wine
2 tbsp sun-dried tomato paste
7 oz/200 g Italian sausage
2 eggs
1⅓ cups freshly grated Parmesan

½ cup fresh breadcrumbs
1½ cups ricotta cheese
8 sheets lasagne, cooked
12 oz/350 g mozzarella cheese, sliced
salt and pepper
chopped fresh parsley, to garnish

Beef Lasagna with Ricotta & Mozzarella

Heat ½ cup of the oil with the butter in a large pan. Add the bacon, onion, celery, and carrot and cook over low heat, until softened. Increase the heat to medium, add the beef, and cook until evenly browned. Stir in the wine and tomato paste, season to taste with salt and pepper, and bring to a boil. Lower the heat, cover, and simmer gently for 1½ hours, until the beef is tender.

Meanwhile, heat 2 tablespoons of the remaining oil in a skillet. Add the sausage and cook for 8–10 minutes. Remove from the skillet and discard the skin. Thinly slice the sausage and set aside.

Transfer the beef to a cutting board and dice finely. Return half the beef to the sauce. Mix the remaining beef in a bowl with 1 egg, 1 tablespoon of the Parmesan, and the breadcrumbs. Shape into walnut-size balls. Heat the remaining oil in a skillet, add the meatballs, and cook for 5–8 minutes, until browned.

Pass the ricotta through a strainer into a bowl. Stir in the remaining egg and 4 tablespoons of the remaining Parmesan.

Preheat the oven to 350°F/180°C. In a rectangular ovenproof dish, make layers with the lasagna sheets, ricotta mixture, meat sauce, meatballs, sausage, and mozzarella. Finish with a layer of the ricotta mixture and sprinkle with the remaining Parmesan. Bake the lasagna in the preheated oven for 20–25 minutes, until cooked through and bubbling. Serve, garnished with parsley.

SERVES 6

1 potato, diced
14 oz/400 g ground beef
1 onion, finely chopped
1 egg
4 tbsp chopped fresh
   flat-leaf parsley

all-purpose flour, for
   dusting
5 tbsp olive oil
1¾ cups strained canned
   tomato sauce
2 tbsp tomato paste
14 oz/400 g dried
   spaghetti

salt and pepper
fresh basil leaves,
   to garnish
shavings of fresh
   Parmesan cheese,
   to garnish

Spaghetti with Meatballs

Place the potato in a small pan, add cold water to cover and a pinch of salt, and bring to a boil. Cook for 10–15 minutes until tender, then drain. Mash thoroughly with either a potato masher or fork, or by passing through a potato ricer.

Combine the potato, beef, onion, egg, and parsley in a bowl and season to taste with salt and pepper. Spread out the flour on a plate. With dampened hands, shape the meat mixture into walnut-size balls and roll in the flour. Shake off any excess.

Heat the olive oil in a heavy-bottom skillet, add the meatballs, and cook over medium heat, stirring and turning frequently, for 8–10 minutes, or until golden all over.

Add the tomato sauce and tomato paste and cook for an additional 10 minutes, or until the sauce is reduced and thickened.

Meanwhile, bring a large pan of lightly salted water to a boil. Add the pasta, return to a boil, and cook for 8–10 minutes, or until tender but still firm to the bite.

Drain well and add to the meatball sauce, tossing well to coat. Transfer to individual warmed dishes, garnish with the basil leaves and Parmesan cheese, and serve immediately.

SERVES 6

3 tbsp olive oil
5 tbsp butter
12 oz/350 g braising beef, in a single piece
1 red onion, finely chopped
1 celery stalk, finely chopped

1 carrot, finely chopped
2/3 cup red wine
1 cup beef stock
1 tbsp tomato paste
1 cup fresh breadcrumbs
4 tbsp freshly grated Parmesan cheese
pinch of freshly grated nutmeg

pinch of ground cinnamon
2 eggs, lightly beaten
1½ quantities Basic Pasta Dough (see p. 6)
all-purpose flour, for dusting
salt and pepper

Beef Ravioli

Heat the oil and half the butter in a large pan. Add the beef and cook over medium heat for 8–10 minutes. Remove the beef from the pan. Lower the heat and add the onion, celery, and carrot to the pan. Cook for 5 minutes, until softened. Return the beef to the pan, add the wine, and cook until reduced by two-thirds. Combine the stock and tomato paste, stir into the pan, and season to taste with salt and pepper. Cover and simmer very gently for 3 hours, until the meat is tender and the sauce has thickened. Remove the beef from the pan and let cool slightly.

Mix the breadcrumbs and half the Parmesan together and stir in about half of the sauce (discard the remaining sauce). Finely chop the beef and stir it into the breadcrumb mixture. Season to taste with salt and pepper and stir in the nutmeg, cinnamon, and eggs.

Roll out the pasta dough on a lightly floured surface to 1/16–1/8 inch/2–3 mm thick. Using a fluted 2-inch/5-cm cookie cutter, stamp out rounds. Place about 1 teaspoon of the beef mixture in the center of each round, brush the edges with water, and fold in half, pressing the edges to seal. Place on a floured dish towel and let stand for 30 minutes.

Bring a pan of salted water to a boil. Add the ravioli and cook for 5–8 minutes, until tender. Meanwhile, melt the remaining butter. Drain the ravioli and divide among individual dishes. Pour the melted butter over the top, sprinkle with the remaining Parmesan, and serve.

SERVES 4

1 lb 10 oz/750 g boneless
  lean lamb in a single
  piece
6 garlic cloves, thinly
  sliced

6–8 fresh rosemary sprigs
½ cup olive oil
14 oz/400 g dried
  tagliatelle
4 tbsp butter

6 oz/175 g white
  mushrooms
salt and pepper
freshly shaved Romano
  cheese, to serve

Tagliatelle with Lamb

Using a sharp knife, cut small pockets all over the lamb, then insert a garlic slice and a few rosemary leaves in each one. Heat 2 tablespoons of the olive oil in a large, heavy-bottom skillet. Add the lamb and cook over medium heat, turning occasionally, for 25–30 minutes, until tender and cooked to your liking.

Meanwhile, chop the remaining rosemary and place in a mortar. Add the remaining oil and pound with a pestle. Season to taste with salt and pepper and set aside.

Remove the lamb from the heat, cover with foil, and let stand. Bring a large pan of salted water to a boil. Add the pasta, bring back to a boil, and cook for 8–10 minutes, until tender but still firm to the bite.

Meanwhile, melt the butter in another pan. Add the mushrooms and cook over medium–low heat, stirring occasionally, for 5–8 minutes, until tender.

Drain the pasta, return it to the pan, and toss with half the rosemary oil. Uncover the lamb and cut it into slices. Divide the tagliatelle among individual warmed plates, season with pepper, and top with the lamb and mushrooms. Drizzle with the remaining rosemary oil, sprinkle with the Romano cheese, and serve immediately.

SERVES 4

1 tbsp olive oil
1 onion, chopped
2 garlic cloves, finely
   chopped
1 lb/450 g fresh ground
   lamb
2 tbsp tomato paste

2 tbsp all-purpose flour
1¼ cups chicken stock
1 tsp ground cinnamon
4 oz/115 g dried
   macaroni
2 beefsteak tomatoes,
   sliced

1¼ cups Greek yogurt
2 eggs, lightly beaten
salt and pepper

Pasticcio

Preheat the oven to 375°F/190°C. Heat the olive oil in a large, heavy-bottom skillet. Add the onion and garlic and cook over low heat, stirring occasionally, for 5 minutes, or until softened. Add the lamb and cook, breaking it up with a wooden spoon, until browned all over. Add the tomato paste and sprinkle in the flour. Cook, stirring, for 1 minute, then stir in the stock. Season to taste with salt and pepper and stir in the cinnamon. Bring to a boil, reduce the heat, cover, and cook for 25 minutes.

Meanwhile, bring a large, heavy-bottom pan of lightly salted water to a boil. Add the pasta, return to a boil, and cook for 8–10 minutes, or until tender but still firm to the bite.

Drain the pasta and stir into the lamb mixture. Spoon into a large ovenproof dish and arrange the tomato slices on top. Beat together the yogurt and eggs, then spoon this over the lamb mixture. Bake in the preheated oven for 1 hour and then serve immediately.

SERVES 4

4 tbsp olive oil
1 red onion, chopped
1 garlic clove, chopped
1 celery stalk, sliced
14 oz/400 g dried
  rigatoni (pasta tubes)

10 oz/280 g chorizo
  sausage, sliced
8 oz/225 g cremini
  mushrooms, halved

1 tbsp chopped fresh
  cilantro
1 tbsp lime juice
salt and pepper

Rigatoni with Chorizo + Mushrooms

Heat the oil in a skillet. Add the onion, garlic, and celery and cook over low heat, stirring occasionally, for 5 minutes, until softened.

Meanwhile, bring a large pan of lightly salted water to a boil. Add the pasta, bring back to a boil, and cook for 8–10 minutes, or until tender but still firm to the bite.

While the pasta is cooking, add the chorizo to the skillet and cook, stirring occasionally, for 5 minutes, until evenly browned. Add the mushrooms and cook, stirring occasionally, for an additional 5 minutes. Stir in the cilantro and lime juice and season to taste with salt and pepper.

Drain the pasta and return it to the pan. Add the chorizo-and-mushroom mixture and toss lightly. Divide among warmed serving dishes and serve immediately.

SERVES 4

3 tbsp olive oil
1 onion, chopped
1 red bell pepper, seeded and diced
1 orange bell pepper, seeded and diced

1 lb 12 oz/800 g canned chopped tomatoes
1 tbsp sun-dried tomato paste
1 tsp paprika
8 oz/225 g pepperoni sausage, sliced

2 tbsp chopped fresh flat-leaf parsley, plus extra to garnish
1 lb/450 g dried penne (pasta quills)
salt and pepper

Pepperoni Pasta

Heat 2 tablespoons of the olive oil in a large, heavy-bottom skillet. Add the onion and cook over low heat, stirring occasionally, for 5 minutes, or until softened. Add the red and orange bell peppers, tomatoes and their can juices, sun-dried tomato paste, and paprika and bring to a boil.

Add the pepperoni and parsley and season to taste with salt and pepper. Stir well, bring to a boil, then reduce the heat and simmer for 10–15 minutes.

Meanwhile, bring a large, heavy-bottom pan of lightly salted water to a boil. Add the pasta, return to a boil, and cook for 8–10 minutes, or until tender but still firm to the bite. Drain well and transfer to a warmed serving dish. Add the remaining olive oil and toss. Add the sauce and toss again. Sprinkle with parsley and serve immediately.

SERVES 4

1 lb/450 g dried
   spaghetti
1 tbsp olive oil

8 oz/225 g rindless
   pancetta or lean
   bacon, chopped
4 eggs

5 tbsp light cream
2 tbsp freshly grated
   Parmesan cheese
salt and pepper

Spaghetti Alla Carbonara

Bring a large, heavy-bottom pan of lightly salted water to a boil. Add the pasta, return to a boil, and cook for 8–10 minutes, or until tender but still firm to the bite.

Meanwhile, heat the olive oil in a heavy-bottom skillet. Add the pancetta and cook over medium heat, stirring frequently, for 8–10 minutes.

Beat the eggs with the cream in a small bowl and season to taste with salt and pepper. Drain the pasta and return it to the pan. Turn into the contents of the skillet, then add the egg mixture and half the Parmesan cheese. Stir well, then transfer to a warmed serving dish. Serve immediately, sprinkled with the remaining cheese.

SERVES 6

1 tbsp olive oil
4 strips lean bacon or
  pancetta
2 cups mushrooms, sliced

2 cups dried fusilli
2 eggs, beaten
1 cup cubed cheddar or
  mozzarella cheese

salt and pepper
chopped fresh flat-leaf
  parsley, to garnish

Fusilli with Bacon, Eggs & Mushrooms

Heat the oil in a skillet over a medium heat. Add the bacon and cook until crisp. Remove with tongs, cut into small pieces, and keep warm.

Cook the mushrooms in the pan with the bacon fat for 5–7 minutes, or until soft. Remove from the heat.

Meanwhile, bring a large pan of lightly salted water to a boil. Add the pasta, bring back to a boil, and cook for 8–10 minutes, or until tender but still firm to the bite. Drain and keep warm.

Stir the mushrooms, beaten eggs, and the cheese cubes into the pasta. Season with pepper and toss until the eggs have coated the pasta and the cheese has melted.

Divide among individual warmed dishes. Sprinkle with the bacon pieces and parsley and serve at once.

SERVES 4

1 cup sour cream
8 oz/225 g cremini
   mushrooms, quartered
14 oz/400 g dried farfalle
   (pasta bows)

3 oz/85 g Gorgonzola
   cheese, crumbled
1 tbsp chopped fresh
   flat-leaf parsley, plus
   extra sprigs to garnish

1 cup diced cooked ham
salt and pepper

Farfalle with Gorgonzola & Ham

Pour the sour cream into a pan, add the mushrooms, and season to taste with salt and pepper. Bring to just below a boil, then lower the heat and simmer very gently, stirring occasionally, for 8–10 minutes, until the cream has thickened.

Meanwhile, bring a large pan of salted water to a boil. Add the pasta, bring back to a boil, and cook for 8–10 minutes, until tender but still firm to the bite.

Remove the pan of mushrooms from the heat and stir in the Gorgonzola until it has melted. Return the pan to very low heat and stir in the parsley and ham.

Drain the pasta and add it to the sauce. Toss lightly, then divide among individual warmed plates, garnish with parsley, and serve.

SERVES 4

2 tbsp olive oil
2 onions, chopped
2 garlic cloves, finely
  chopped
1 tbsp shredded fresh
  basil

1 lb 12 oz/800 g canned
  chopped tomatoes
1 tbsp tomato paste
10–12 dried cannelloni
  tubes
butter, for greasing
1 cup ricotta cheese

¾ cup diced cooked
  ham
1 egg
½ cup freshly grated
  Romano cheese
salt and pepper

Cannelloni with Ham + Ricotta

Preheat the oven to 350°F/180°C. Heat the olive oil in a large, heavy-bottom skillet. Add the onions and garlic and cook over low heat, stirring occasionally, for 5 minutes, or until the onion is softened. Add the basil, chopped tomatoes and their can juices, and tomato paste, and season to taste with salt and pepper. Reduce the heat and simmer for 30 minutes, or until thickened.

Meanwhile, bring a large, heavy-bottom pan of lightly salted water to a boil. Add the cannelloni tubes, return to a boil, and cook for 8–10 minutes, or until tender but still firm to the bite. Using a slotted spoon, transfer the cannelloni tubes to a large plate and pat dry with paper towels.

Grease a large, shallow ovenproof dish with butter. Mix the ricotta, ham, and egg together in a bowl and season to taste with salt and pepper. Using a teaspoon, fill the cannelloni tubes with the ricotta mixture and place in a single layer in the prepared dish. Pour the tomato sauce over the cannelloni and sprinkle with the grated Romano cheese. Bake in the preheated oven for 30 minutes, or until golden brown. Serve immediately.

SERVES 4

1 tbsp olive oil
2 tbsp butter
1 onion, finely chopped
2/3 cup diced cooked
  ham
2 garlic cloves, very finely
  chopped

1 red chile, seeded and
  finely chopped
1 lb 12 oz/800 g canned
  chopped tomatoes
1 lb/450 g dried penne
  (pasta quills)

2 tbsp chopped fresh
  flat-leaf parsley
salt and pepper
6 tbsp freshly grated
  Parmesan cheese

Penne with Ham, Tomato + Chili Sauce

Put the olive oil and 1 tablespoon of the butter in a large skillet over medium–low heat. Add the onion and cook for 10 minutes, or until soft and golden. Add the ham and cook for an additional 5 minutes, or until lightly browned. Stir in the garlic, chile, and tomatoes. Season to taste with salt and pepper. Bring to a boil, then simmer over medium–low heat for 30–40 minutes, or until thickened.

Meanwhile, bring a large pan of lightly salted water to a boil. Add the pasta, bring back to a boil, and cook for 8–10 minutes, or until tender but still firm to the bite. Drain and keep warm.

Pour the sauce over the pasta. Add the parsley, Parmesan cheese, and the remaining butter. Toss well to mix and serve immediately.

SERVES 4

1 lb/450 g pork
   tenderloin, thinly sliced
4 tbsp olive oil
8 oz/225 g white
   mushrooms, sliced
1 tbsp lemon juice
pinch of saffron threads

12 oz/350 g dried
   orecchiette
   (ear-shaped pasta)
4 tbsp heavy cream
salt
12 quail eggs

red wine sauce
1 tbsp olive oil
1 onion, chopped
1 tbsp tomato paste
¾ cup red wine
1 tbsp finely chopped
   fresh oregano

Pasta & Pork in Cream Sauce

To make the red wine sauce, heat the oil in a small, heavy-bottom pan, add the onion, and cook until transparent. Stir in the tomato paste, red wine, and oregano. Heat gently to reduce and set aside.

Pound the slices of pork between 2 sheets of plastic wrap until wafer thin, then cut into strips. Heat the oil in a skillet, add the pork, and cook for 5 minutes. Add the mushrooms and cook for an additional 2 minutes. Strain and pour in the red wine sauce. Reduce the heat and simmer for 20 minutes.

Meanwhile, bring a large, heavy-bottom pan of lightly salted water to a boil. Add the lemon juice, saffron, and pasta, return to a boil, and cook for 8–10 minutes, or until tender but still firm to the bite. Drain the pasta thoroughly, return to the pan, and keep warm. Stir the cream into the pan with the pork and heat for a few minutes.

Boil the quail eggs for 3 minutes, cool them in cold water, and remove the shells. Divide the pasta among individual warmed plates, top with the pork and the sauce, and garnish with the eggs. Serve immediately.

SERVES 4

1 lb/450 g dried
tagliatelle
3 tbsp peanut oil
12 oz/350 g pork
tenderloin, cut into
thin strips
1 garlic clove, finely
chopped
1 bunch of scallions,
sliced

1-inch/2.5-cm piece fresh
ginger, grated
2 fresh Thai chiles, seeded
and finely chopped
1 red bell pepper, seeded
and cut into thin sticks
1 yellow bell pepper,
seeded and cut into
thin sticks
3 zucchini cut into thin
sticks

2 tbsp finely chopped
peanuts
1 tsp ground cinnamon
1 tbsp oyster sauce
2 oz/55 g creamed
coconut, grated
salt and pepper
2 tbsp chopped fresh
cilantro, to garnish

Chili Pork with Tagliatelle

Bring a large, heavy-bottom pan of lightly salted water to a boil. Add the pasta, return to a boil, and cook for 8–10 minutes, or until tender but still firm to the bite.

Meanwhile, heat the peanut oil in a preheated wok or large, heavy-bottom skillet. Add the pork and stir-fry for 5 minutes. Add the garlic, scallions, ginger, and Thai chiles, and stir-fry for 2 minutes.

Add the bell peppers and zucchini and stir-fry for 1 minute. Add the peanuts, cinnamon, oyster sauce, and creamed coconut and stir-fry for an additional 1 minute. Season to taste with salt and pepper. Drain the pasta and divide among individual dishes. Top with the chili pork, sprinkle with the chopped cilantro, and serve.

SERVES 4

2 tbsp olive oil
1 onion, chopped
1 garlic clove, finely
  chopped
2 carrots, diced
2 oz/55 g pancetta,
  chopped
4 oz/115 g mushrooms,
  chopped

1 lb/450 g fresh ground
  pork
½ cup dry white wine
4 tbsp canned tomato
  sauce
7 oz/200 g canned
  chopped tomatoes
2 tsp chopped fresh
  sage, plus extra sprigs
  to garnish

8 oz/225 g dried penne
  (pasta quills)
5 oz/140 g mozzarella
  cheese, diced
4 tbsp freshly grated
  Parmesan
1¼ cups hot, store-bought
  béchamel sauce
salt and pepper

Pork & Pasta Casserole

Preheat the oven to 400°F/200°C. Heat the olive oil in a large, heavy-bottom skillet. Add the onion, garlic, and carrots, and cook over low heat, stirring occasionally, for 5 minutes, or until the onion has softened. Add the pancetta and cook for 5 minutes. Add the chopped mushrooms and cook, stirring occasionally, for an additional 2 minutes. Add the ground pork and cook, breaking it up with a wooden spoon, until the meat is browned all over. Stir in the wine, tomato sauce, chopped tomatoes and their can juices, and the chopped sage. Season to taste with salt and pepper, bring to a boil, then cover and simmer over low heat for 25–30 minutes.

Meanwhile, bring a large, heavy-bottom pan of lightly salted water to a boil. Add the pasta, return to a boil, and cook for 8–10 minutes, or until tender but still firm to the bite.

Spoon the pork mixture into a large ovenproof dish. Stir the mozzarella and half the Parmesan into the béchamel sauce. Drain the pasta and stir the sauce into it, then spoon it over the pork mixture. Sprinkle with the remaining Parmesan and bake in the preheated oven for 25–30 minutes, or until golden brown. Serve immediately, garnished with sage sprigs.

SERVES 6

2 tbsp olive oil
2 lb/900 g fresh ground chicken
1 garlic clove, finely chopped
4 carrots, chopped

4 leeks, sliced
2 cups chicken stock
2 tbsp tomato paste
8 lasagna sheets, cooked
1 cup shredded cheddar cheese

1 tsp Dijon mustard
2½ cups hot, store-bought béchamel sauce
salt and pepper

Chicken Lasagna

Preheat the oven to 375°F/190°C. Heat the oil in a heavy-bottom pan. Add the chicken and cook over medium heat, breaking it up with a wooden spoon, for 5 minutes, or until it is browned all over. Add the garlic, carrots, and leeks, and cook, stirring occasionally, for 5 minutes.

Stir in the chicken stock and tomato paste and season to taste with salt and pepper. Bring to a boil, reduce the heat, cover, and simmer for 30 minutes.

Whisk half the cheddar cheese and the mustard into the hot béchamel sauce. In a large ovenproof dish, make alternate layers of the chicken mixture, lasagna sheets, and cheese sauce, ending with a layer of cheese sauce. Sprinkle with the remaining cheddar cheese and bake in the preheated oven for 1 hour, or until golden brown and bubbling. Serve immediately.

SERVES 4

2 tbsp olive oil
1 lb/450 g skinless, boneless chicken breasts, cut into thin strips

6 scallions, chopped
8 oz/225 g feta cheese, diced
4 tbsp snipped fresh chives

1 lb/450 g dried penne (pasta quills)
salt and pepper

Penne with Chicken & Feta Cheese

Heat the olive oil in a heavy-bottom skillet. Add the chicken and cook over medium heat, stirring frequently, for 5–8 minutes, or until golden all over and cooked through. Add the scallions and cook for 2 minutes. Stir the feta cheese into the skillet with half the chives and season to taste with salt and pepper.

Meanwhile, bring a large, heavy-bottom pan of lightly salted water to a boil. Add the pasta, return to a boil, and cook for 8–10 minutes, or until tender but still firm to the bite. Drain well, then transfer to a warmed serving dish.

Spoon the chicken mixture onto the pasta, toss lightly, and serve immediately, garnished with the remaining chives.

SERVES 4

1 tbsp olive oil
thinly pared rind of
   1 lemon, cut into
   julienne strips
1 tsp finely chopped fresh
   ginger
1 tsp sugar

1 cup chicken stock
9 oz/250 g dried
   spaghetti
4 tbsp butter
8 oz/225 g skinless,
   boneless chicken
   breasts, diced

1 red onion, finely
   chopped
leaves from 2 bunches of
   flat-leaf parsley
salt

Spaghetti with Parsley Chicken

Heat the olive oil in a heavy-bottom pan. Add the lemon rind and cook over low heat, stirring frequently, for 5 minutes. Stir in the ginger and sugar, season to taste with salt, and cook, stirring constantly, for an additional 2 minutes. Pour in the chicken stock, bring to a boil, then cook for 5 minutes, or until the liquid has reduced by half.

Meanwhile, bring a large, heavy-bottom pan of lightly salted water to a boil. Add the pasta, return to a boil, and cook for 8–10 minutes, or until tender but still firm to the bite.

Melt half the butter in a skillet. Add the chicken and onion and cook, stirring frequently, for 5 minutes, or until the chicken is lightly browned all over. Stir in the lemon-and-ginger mixture and cook for 1 minute. Stir in the parsley leaves and cook, stirring constantly, for an additional 3 minutes.

Drain the pasta and transfer to a warmed serving dish, then add the remaining butter and toss well. Add the chicken sauce, toss again, and serve.

SERVES 4

4 oz/115 g boned
    chicken breast, skinned
2 oz/55 g prosciutto
1½ oz/40 g cooked
    spinach, well drained
1 tbsp finely chopped
    onion
6 tbsp freshly grated
    Parmesan cheese

pinch of ground allspice
2 eggs, beaten
2 quantities Basic Pasta
    Dough (see p. 6)
all-purpose flour, for
    dusting
1¼ cups light cream
2 garlic cloves, crushed

4 oz/115 g white
    mushrooms, thinly
    sliced
salt and pepper
2 tbsp chopped fresh
    parsley, to garnish

Chicken Tortellini

Bring a pan of salted water to a boil. Add the chicken and poach for about
10 minutes. Let cool slightly, then place in a food processor with the prosciutto,
spinach, and onion and process until finely chopped. Stir in 2 tablespoons of the
Parmesan, the allspice, and half the eggs and season with salt and pepper.

Roll out the pasta dough on a lightly floured counter to a rectangle ¹⁄₁₆–⅛ inch/
2–3 mm thick. Using a 2-inch/5-cm plain cookie cutter, stamp out rounds. Place
about 1 teaspoon of the filling in the center of each round. Brush the edges with a
little beaten egg, then fold in half to make a half moon, pressing the edges to seal.
Wrap the half moon around the tip of your index finger until the corners meet and
press them together to seal. Repeat with the remaining pasta half moons. Place the
filled tortellini on a floured dish towel and let stand for 1 hour.

Bring a pan of lightly salted water to a boil. Add the tortellini in batches and cook
for 10 minutes. Remove with a slotted spoon and drain on paper towels, then
transfer to a serving dish.

To make the sauce, bring the cream and garlic to a boil in a small pan, then
simmer for 3 minutes. Add the mushrooms and 2 tablespoons of the Parmesan
cheese, season to taste with salt and pepper, and simmer for 2–3 minutes. Pour the
sauce over the tortellini. Sprinkle the remaining Parmesan cheese on top, garnish
with the parsley, and serve.

SERVES 4

butter, for greasing
2 tbsp olive oil
2 garlic cloves, crushed
1 large onion, finely chopped
8 oz/225 g wild mushrooms, sliced
1½ cups fresh ground chicken

4 oz/115 g prosciutto, diced
⅔ cup Marsala wine
7 oz/200 g canned chopped tomatoes
1 tbsp shredded fresh basil leaves
2 tbsp tomato paste

10–12 dried cannelloni tubes
2½ cups store-bought béchamel sauce
¾ cup freshly grated Parmesan cheese
salt and pepper
chopped flat-leaf parsley, to garnish

Chicken & Mushroom Cannelloni

Preheat the oven to 375°F/190°C. Lightly grease a large ovenproof dish. Heat the olive oil in a heavy-bottom skillet. Add the garlic, onion, and mushrooms, and cook over low heat, stirring frequently, for 8–10 minutes. Add the ground chicken and prosciutto and cook, stirring frequently, for 12 minutes, or until browned all over. Stir in the Marsala, tomatoes and their can juices, basil, and tomato paste, and cook for 4 minutes. Season to taste with salt and pepper, then cover and simmer for 30 minutes. Uncover, stir, and simmer for 15 minutes.

Meanwhile, bring a large, heavy-bottom pan of lightly salted water to a boil. Add the pasta, return to a boil, and cook for 8–10 minutes, or until tender but still firm to the bite. Using a slotted spoon, transfer the cannelloni tubes to a plate and pat dry with paper towels.

Using a teaspoon, fill the cannelloni tubes with the chicken-and-mushroom mixture. Transfer them to the dish. Pour the béchamel sauce over them to cover completely and sprinkle with the grated Parmesan cheese.

Bake in the preheated oven for 30 minutes, or until golden brown and bubbling. Serve immediately, garnished with parsley.

SERVES 4

1 lb/450 g turkey steaks
grated zest of 1 lemon
2 tsp cracked black
   peppercorns

12 oz/350 g egg
   tagliatelle
1 tbsp olive oil
4½ tbsp butter
juice of ½ lemon

1 cup heavy cream
4 tbsp chopped flat-leaf
   parsley
salt

Turkey Tagliatelle with Lemon Pepper Cream Sauce

Place the turkey steaks between two sheets of plastic wrap and flatten with a mallet. Slice the meat across the grain into thin strips measuring ½ x 3½ inches/ 1 x 9 cm. Put the strips in a shallow dish and toss with the lemon zest and the cracked peppercorns.

Bring a large pan of lightly salted water to a boil. Add the pasta, bring back to a boil, and cook for 8–10 minutes, or until tender but still firm to the bite.

Meanwhile, heat a large skillet over medium–high heat. Add the oil and half the butter and pan-fry the turkey strips for 5 minutes, until no longer pink. Season with salt to taste, then transfer to a plate and keep warm.

Add the remaining butter to the pan. Stir in the lemon juice and simmer for a few seconds. Pour in the cream, bring to a boil, then reduce the heat and simmer for 5 minutes, stirring often. Return the turkey to the pan, stirring until well coated with the cream.

Drain the pasta, reserving 4 tablespoons of the cooking water. Turn the pasta into a warmed serving dish. Stir the cooking water into the turkey mixture, then add the parsley. Pour the sauce over the pasta, and toss to mix. Serve immediately.

SERVES 4

4 oz/115 g dried short macaroni
1 small egg, lightly beaten
2 tbsp butter
4 small leeks, green part included, finely sliced
2 carrots, diced

1 tbsp all-purpose flour
¼ tsp freshly grated nutmeg
9 fl oz/250 ml chicken stock
8 oz/225 g diced cooked turkey or chicken

2 oz/55 g diced cooked ham
3 tbsp chopped fresh flat-leaf parsley
1 cup freshly shredded Gruyère cheese
salt and pepper

Turkey, Leek & Cheese Casserole

Preheat the oven to 350°F/180°C. Bring a large pan of lightly salted water to a boil. Add the pasta, bring back to a boil, and cook for 8–10 minutes, or until tender but still firm to the bite. Drain the pasta and return to the pan. Stir in the egg and a pat of the butter, mixing well. Set aside.

Melt the remaining butter in a saucepan over medium heat. Add the leeks and carrots. Cover and cook for 5 minutes, shaking the saucepan occasionally, until just tender.

Add the flour and nutmeg. Cook for 1 minute, stirring constantly. Pour in the stock. Bring to a boil, stirring constantly. Stir in the turkey, ham, and parsley. Season to taste with salt and pepper.

Spread half the turkey mixture over the bottom of a shallow baking dish. Spread the macaroni over the turkey. Top with the remaining turkey mixture. Sprinkle with the cheese. Bake in the oven for 15–20 minutes. Serve the casserole when the cheese is golden and bubbling.

SERVES 4

12 oz/350 g ground turkey

1 small garlic clove, finely chopped

2 tbsp finely chopped fresh parsley

1 egg, lightly beaten

all-purpose flour, for dusting

3 tbsp olive oil

1 onion, finely chopped

1 celery stalk, finely chopped

1 carrot, finely chopped

14 oz/400 g canned tomato sauce

1 fresh rosemary sprig

1 bay leaf

12 oz/350 g dried penne (pasta quills)

salt and pepper

freshly grated Parmesan cheese, to serve

Penne with Turkey Meatballs

Put the turkey, garlic, and parsley in a bowl and mix well. Stir in the egg and season to taste with salt and pepper. Dust your hands lightly with flour and shape the mixture into walnut-size balls between your palms. Lightly dust each meatball with flour.

Heat the olive oil in a pan. Add the onion, celery, and carrot and cook over low heat, stirring occasionally, for 5 minutes, until softened. Increase the heat to medium, add the meatballs, and cook, turning frequently, for 8–10 minutes, until golden brown all over.

Pour in the tomato sauce, add the rosemary and bay leaf, season to taste with salt and pepper, and bring to a boil. Lower the heat, cover, and simmer gently, stirring occasionally, for 40–45 minutes. Remove and discard the herbs.

Shortly before the meatballs are ready, bring a large pan of salted water to a boil. Add the pasta, bring back to a boil, and cook for 8–10 minutes, until tender but still firm to the bite. Drain and add to the pan with the meatballs. Stir gently and heat through briefly, then spoon onto individual warmed plates. Sprinkle generously with Parmesan and serve immediately.

SERVES 3–4

4 duck legs, halved
½ cup good-quality balsamic vinegar
2 tbsp olive oil, for frying
1 onion, finely chopped
1 carrot, finely chopped
1 celery stalk, finely chopped

1 large garlic clove, finely chopped
1 cup thinly sliced cremini mushrooms
1¾ cups chicken stock
1 tbsp tomato paste
½ tsp dried oregano

squeeze of lemon juice
4 tbsp chopped flat-leaf parsley
12 oz/350 g conchiglie
salt and pepper

Conchiglie with Balsamic-Glazed Duck & Mushrooms

Remove the skin from the duck legs and discard. Place the joints in a skillet and pour in the balsamic vinegar, simmer, and turn frequently for 10 minutes. Reduce the heat for 5 minutes then remove the pan from the heat and set aside. Heat the oil in a saucepan and add the onion, carrot, celery, and garlic and gently fry over medium heat until soft but not colored. Stir in the mushrooms, season with salt and pepper, and cook for an additional 5 minutes, and then place the duck joints on top of the vegetables.

Pour the stock over the duck and stir in the tomato paste and oregano. Cover and bring to a boil, then reduce the heat and simmer gently for 45–60 minutes, stirring occasionally, until the duck is tender.

Remove the duck from the pan, using tongs. Simmer the sauce for a few minutes until slightly thickened and reduced. Strip the duck meat from the bones, chop it into small pieces, and put back in the pan. Add a squeeze of lemon juice, the parsley, and season to taste with salt and pepper. Simmer gently for 5 minutes to heat through.

Bring a large pan of lightly salted water to a boil. Add the pasta, return to the boil, and cook for 8–10 minutes, or until tender but still firm to the bite. Drain and transfer to a warmed serving dish. Toss with the sauce and serve immediately.

SERVES 4

4 tbsp olive oil
4 duck legs
1 shallot, finely chopped
1 leek, white part only, finely chopped
1 garlic clove, finely chopped
1 celery stalk, finely chopped

1 carrot, finely chopped
4 pancetta or bacon strips, diced
1 tbsp chopped fresh parsley
1 bay leaf
5 tbsp dry white wine
14 oz/400 g canned chopped tomatoes

2 tbsp tomato paste
pinch of sugar
1 lb/450 g dried fettuccine
salt and pepper
freshly grated Parmesan cheese, to serve

Fettuccine with Duck Sauce

Heat half the oil in a heavy skillet. Add the duck and cook over medium heat, turning frequently, for 8–10 minutes, until golden brown all over. Using a slotted spoon, transfer to a large pan.

Wipe out the skillet with paper towels, then add the remaining oil. Add the shallot, leek, garlic, celery, carrot, and pancetta and cook over low heat, stirring occasionally, for 10 minutes. Using a slotted spoon, transfer the mixture to the pan with the duck and stir in the parsley. Add the bay leaf and season to taste with salt and pepper.

Pour in the wine and cook over high heat, stirring occasionally, until reduced by half. Add the tomatoes, tomato paste, and sugar and cook for an additional 5 minutes. Pour in enough water to cover and bring to a boil. Lower the heat, cover, and simmer gently for 1 hour, until the duck legs are cooked through and tender.

Remove the pan from the heat and transfer the duck legs to a cutting board. Skim off the fat from the surface of the sauce and discard the bay leaf. Remove and discard the skin from the duck and cut the meat off the bones, then dice neatly. Return the duck meat to the pan and keep warm.

Bring a large pan of salted water to a boil. Add the pasta, bring back to a boil, and cook for 8–10 minutes, until tender but still firm to the bite. Drain and divide the pasta among individual warmed plates. Taste and adjust the seasoning of the sauce, if necessary, then spoon it on top of the pasta. Sprinkle generously with Parmesan cheese and serve.

Fish & Seafood

SERVES 4

12 oz/350 g dried linguine
2 tbsp olive oil

1 garlic clove, finely chopped
4 oz/115 g smoked salmon, cut into thin strips

2 oz/55 g arugula
salt and pepper

Linguine with Smoked Salmon & Arugula

Bring a large pan of lightly salted water to a boil. Add the pasta, bring back to a boil, and cook for 8–10 minutes, or until tender but still firm to the bite.

Just before the end of the cooking time, heat the olive oil in a heavy-bottom skillet. Add the garlic and cook over a low heat for 1 minute, stirring constantly. Do not let the garlic brown or it will taste bitter. Add the salmon and arugula. Season to taste with salt and pepper and cook for 1 minute, stirring constantly. Remove the skillet from the heat.

Drain the pasta and divide among individual warmed dishes. Add the smoked salmon-and-arugula mixture, toss lightly, and serve immediately.

SERVES 4

14 oz/400 g pasta shells, bows, or tagliatelle
8 oz/225 g broccoli florets
1 tbsp olive oil

2 tbsp butter
1 leek, finely chopped
1 cup garlic and herb cream cheese

6 tbsp whole milk
3½ oz/100 g smoked salmon pieces
salt and pepper

Creamy Smoked Salmon & Broccoli Pasta

Bring a pan of lightly salted water to a boil over medium heat. Add the pasta and cook for 8–10 minutes, or until tender but still firm to the bite. Drain and set aside. Meanwhile, steam the broccoli for 8–10 minutes, or until tender.

At the same time, prepare the sauce. Heat the oil and butter in a small heavy-bottom skillet, then add the leek and sauté for 7 minutes, or until softened. Gently stir in the cream cheese and milk and heat through.

Add the smoked salmon pieces and cook for a minute or so, until they turn opaque. Combine the sauce with the pasta and broccoli and mix together well. Season to taste with salt and pepper and serve immediately.

SERVES 4

1 lb/450 g dried
conchiglie
(pasta shells)
1¼ cups sour cream
2 tsp Dijon mustard

4 large scallions, sliced
finely
8 oz/225 g smoked
salmon, cut into
bite-size pieces

finely grated rind of
½ lemon
salt and pepper
2 tbsp snipped fresh
chives, to garnish

Conchiglie with Smoked Salmon & Sour Cream

Bring a large pan of lightly salted water to a boil. Add the pasta, bring back to a boil, and cook for 8–10 minutes, or until tender but still firm to the bite. Drain and return to the pan.

Add the sour cream, mustard, scallions, smoked salmon, and lemon rind to the pasta. Stir over low heat until heated through. Season to taste with pepper.

Divide the mixture among individual plates, sprinkle with the chives, and serve.

SERVES 6

5 tbsp butter, plus extra for greasing
12 oz/350 g dried spaghetti
7 oz/200 g smoked salmon, cut into strips

10 oz/280 g large cooked shrimp, shelled and deveined
1¼ cups store-bought béchamel sauce

1 cup freshly grated Parmesan cheese
salt
arugula, to garnish

Layered Salmon & Shrimp Spaghetti

Preheat the oven to 350°F/180°C. Butter a large ovenproof dish and set aside.

Bring a large pan of lightly salted water to a boil. Add the pasta, bring back to a boil, and cook for 8–10 minutes, until tender but still firm to the bite. Drain well, return to the pan, add 4 tablespoons of the butter, and toss well.

Spoon half the spaghetti into the prepared dish, cover with the strips of smoked salmon, then top with the shrimp. Pour half the béchamel sauce on top and sprinkle with half the Parmesan. Add the remaining spaghetti, cover with the remaining sauce, and sprinkle with the remaining Parmesan. Dice the remaining butter and dot it over the surface.

Bake in the preheated oven for 15 minutes, until the top is golden. Serve immediately, garnished with arugula.

SERVES 4

8 dried green lasagna
   sheets
2 tbsp butter
1 onion, sliced
½ red bell pepper,
   seeded and chopped
1 zucchini, diced
1 tsp chopped fresh
   ginger

4½ oz/125 g oyster
   mushrooms, torn into
   pieces
8 oz/225 g salmon fillet,
   skinned and cut into
   chunks
3 tbsp dry sherry
2 tsp cornstarch
corn oil, for brushing

3 tbsp all-purpose flour
2 cups milk
¼ cup finely shredded
   cheddar cheese
1 tbsp fresh white
   breadcrumbs
salt and pepper
salad greens, to serve

Salmon Lasagna Rolls

Preheat the over to 400°F/200°C. Cook the lasagna in a large pan of boiling water for 6 minutes, or according to the instructions on the package. Remove with tongs and drain on a clean dish towel.

Melt 1 tablespoon of the butter in a pan. Add the onion and cook over low heat, stirring occasionally, for 5 minutes, until softened. Add the bell pepper, zucchini, and ginger and cook, stirring occasionally, for 10 minutes. Add the mushrooms and salmon and cook for 2 minutes, then combine the sherry and cornstarch and stir into the pan. Cook for an additional 4 minutes, until the fish is opaque and flakes easily. Season to taste with salt and pepper and remove the pan from the heat.

Brush an ovenproof dish with oil and set aside. Melt the remaining butter in another pan. Stir in the flour and cook, stirring constantly, for 2 minutes. Gradually stir in the milk, then cook, stirring constantly, for 10 minutes. Remove the pan from the heat, stir in half the cheese, and season to taste with salt and pepper.

Spoon the salmon filling along one of the shorter sides of each sheet of lasagna. Roll up and place in the prepared dish. Pour the sauce over the rolls and sprinkle with the breadcrumbs and remaining cheese. Bake for 15–20 minutes, until the topping is golden and bubbling. Serve immediately with salad greens.

SERVES 4-6

3 oz/85 g penne or macaroni

2 tsp olive oil, plus extra for coating pasta

1 egg

1 small onion, finely chopped

1 small celery stalk, finely chopped

1 small carrot, peeled and finely chopped

small handful of spinach leaves, tough stalks removed and finely shredded

½ cup milk

2 tbsp heavy cream

¼ cup shredded sharp cheddar cheese

½ tsp English mustard

3¼ oz/90 g undyed smoked flounder, skinned and boned

5 oz/140 g halibut, skinned and boned

⅔ cup diced mozzarella cheese

Two-Fish Casserole

Preheat the oven to 400°F/200°C. Bring a pan of lightly salted water to a boil over medium heat. Add the pasta and cook for 8–10 minutes, or until tender but still firm to the bite. Drain well and toss in oil.

Bring a small saucepan of water to a boil and add the egg. Cook for 8–10 minutes, until the egg is hard boiled. Cool the egg under cold running water.

Heat the oil in a heavy-bottom skillet. Add the onion and sauté for 5 minutes, until softened, then add the celery and carrot and sauté for 3 minutes. Add the spinach and cook for another 2 minutes, until tender.

Stir in the milk and cream and bring to a boil. Turn off the heat and stir in the cheddar cheese and mustard.

Place the fish in a small ovenproof dish. Shell and chop the hard-boiled egg and spoon it over the fish, then top with the sauce. Arrange the pasta over the top and sprinkle with the mozzarella cheese. Bake for 20–25 minutes, until browned on top.

SERVES 6

2 carrots, cut into thin batons
2 celery stalks, cut into thin batons
1 zucchini, cut into thin batons
1 leek, cut into thin batons

4 oz/115 g fresh or frozen peas
5 fl oz/150 ml vegetable stock
8 oz/225 g smoked trout fillets, skinned and cut into thin strips
7 oz/200 g cream cheese

5 fl oz/150 ml dry white wine
2 tbsp chopped fresh dill, plus extra sprigs to garnish
8 oz/225 g dried tagliatelle
salt and pepper

Creamy Smoked Trout Tagliatelle

Put the carrots, celery, zucchini, leek, and peas in a heavy-bottom pan and pour in the stock. Bring to a boil, then reduce the heat and simmer for 5 minutes, or until the vegetables are tender and most of the stock has evaporated. Remove the pan from the heat, stir in the smoked trout, and cover to keep warm.

Put the cheese and wine in a separate large, heavy-bottom pan over a low heat and stir until the cheese has melted and the mixture is smooth. Stir in the chopped dill and season to taste with salt and pepper.

Meanwhile, bring another large, heavy-bottom pan of lightly salted water to the boil. Add the pasta, return to a boil, and cook for 8–10 minutes, until the pasta is tender but still firm to the bite. Drain the pasta and turn into the cheese sauce. Toss the pasta using 2 large forks, then transfer to individual warmed dishes. Top with the smoked trout mixture, garnish with the dill sprigs, and serve immediately.

SERVES 6

1 tbsp all-purpose flour
1 lb/450 g lemon sole
 fillets, skinned and cut
 into chunks
1 lb/450 g monkfish fillets,
 skinned and cut into
 chunks

6 tbsp butter
4 shallots, finely chopped
2 garlic cloves, crushed
1 carrot, diced
1 leek, finely chopped
1¼ cups fish stock
1¼ cups dry white wine

2 tsp Thai fish sauce
1 tbsp balsamic vinegar
1 lb/450 g dried
 fettuccine
salt and pepper
chopped fresh flat-leaf
 parsley, to garnish

Fettuccine with Sole & Monkfish

Season the flour with salt and pepper and spread out on a plate. Coat all the fish pieces with it, shaking off the excess. Melt the butter in a heavy-bottom pan or flameproof casserole. Add the fish, shallots, garlic, carrot, and leek, then cook over low heat, stirring frequently, for 10 minutes. Sprinkle in the remaining seasoned flour and cook, stirring constantly, for 1 minute.

Mix the fish stock, wine, Thai fish sauce, and balsamic vinegar together in a pitcher and gradually stir into the fish mixture. Bring to a boil, stirring constantly, then reduce the heat and simmer gently for 15 minutes.

Meanwhile, bring a large, heavy-bottom pan of lightly salted water to a boil. Add the pasta, return to a boil, and cook for 8–10 minutes, or until tender but still firm to the bite. Drain and divide among individual warmed dishes. Spoon the fish mixture onto the pasta, garnish with chopped parsley, and serve immediately.

SERVES 4

1²/₃ cups small broccoli
  florets
3 tbsp olive oil
12 oz/350 g monkfish
  fillet, skinned and cut
  into bite-size pieces

2 garlic cloves, crushed
½ cup dry white wine
1 cup heavy cream
14 oz/400 g dried fusilli
  (pasta spirals)

3 oz/85 g Gorgonzola
  cheese, diced
salt and pepper

Fusilli with Monkfish & Broccoli

Bring a pan of lightly salted water to a boil, add the broccoli, and cook for
2 minutes. Drain and refresh under cold running water.

Heat the olive oil in a large, heavy-bottom skillet. Add the monkfish and garlic and
season to taste with salt and pepper. Cook, stirring frequently, for 5 minutes, or until
the fish is opaque. Pour in the white wine and cream and cook, stirring occasionally,
for 5 minutes, or until the fish is cooked through and the sauce has thickened. Stir in
the broccoli.

Meanwhile, bring a large, heavy-bottom pan of lightly salted water to a boil. Add
the pasta, return to a boil, and cook for 8–10 minutes, or until tender but still firm to
the bite. Drain and turn the pasta into the pan with the fish, add the cheese, and
toss lightly. Serve immediately.

SERVES 3

3 halibut steaks, weighing about 7 oz/200 g each, boned and skinned
7 oz/200 g egg fettuccine
6 tbsp olive oil

2 tbsp butter
½ onion, thinly sliced
1 large garlic clove, finely chopped
1½ tbsp capers, drained and rinsed

1 charbroiled red bell pepper, cut into squares
salt and pepper
1 tbsp chopped flat-leaf parsley

Fettuccine with Halibut & Roasted Bell Peppers

Cut the halibut into ¾-inch/2-cm cubes. Pat dry with paper towels and put in a shallow dish. Sprinkle with 1 teaspoon of salt, turning to coat, and set aside.

Bring a large pan of lightly salted water to a boil over medium heat. Add the pasta and cook for 8–10 minutes, or until tender but still firm to the bite. Drain and set aside.

Meanwhile, heat a large skillet over medium–high heat. Add the oil and butter, and pan-fry the halibut for 2 minutes, turning carefully, until opaque. Season to taste with pepper, then remove to a plate and set aside.

Reduce the heat to medium–low, and gently cook the onion until softened and beginning to color at the edges. Add the garlic and cook for another 30 seconds, then stir in the capers and bell pepper. Season to taste with salt and pepper. Return the halibut to the pan and heat through.

Drain the pasta and divide among individual warmed plates. Spoon the halibut mixture over the top and sprinkle with the parsley. Serve immediately.

SERVES 4

2 lb/900 g fresh baby
spinach leaves
14 oz/400 g dried
fettuccine

5 tbsp olive oil
3 tbsp pine nuts
3 garlic cloves, crushed

8 canned anchovy fillets,
drained and chopped
salt

Spinach & Anchovy Pasta

Trim off any tough spinach stalks. Rinse the spinach leaves under cold running water and place them in a large pan with only the water that is clinging to them after washing. Cover and cook over high heat, shaking the pan from time to time, until the spinach has wilted but retains its color. Drain well, set aside, and keep warm.

Bring a large, heavy-bottom pan of lightly salted water to a boil. Add the pasta, return to a boil, and cook for 8–10 minutes, or until tender but still firm to the bite.

Meanwhile, heat 4 tablespoons of the olive oil in a separate pan. Add the pine nuts and cook until golden. Remove the pine nuts from the pan and set aside until needed.

Add the garlic to the pan and cook until golden. Add the anchovies and stir in the spinach. Cook, stirring, for 2–3 minutes, until heated through. Return the pine nuts to the pan.

Drain the fettuccine, toss in the remaining olive oil, and transfer to a warmed serving dish. Spoon the anchovy and spinach sauce over the fettuccine, toss lightly, and serve immediately.

SERVES 4

3 tbsp olive oil
2 garlic cloves, finely
   chopped
10 canned anchovy
   fillets, drained and
   chopped

1 cup black olives, pitted
   and chopped
1 tbsp capers, drained
   and rinsed
1 lb/450 g plum
   tomatoes, peeled,
   seeded, and chopped

pinch of cayenne pepper
14 oz/400 g dried
   spaghetti
salt
2 tbsp chopped fresh
   parsley, to garnish

Spaghetti Alla Puttanesca

Heat the olive oil in a heavy-bottom skillet. Add the garlic and cook over low heat, stirring frequently, for 2 minutes. Add the anchovies and mash them to a pulp with a fork. Add the olives, capers, and tomatoes, and season to taste with cayenne pepper. Cover and simmer for 25 minutes.

Meanwhile, bring a large, heavy-bottom pan of lightly salted water to a boil. Add the pasta, return to a boil, and cook for 8–10 minutes, or until tender but still firm to the bite. Drain well and transfer to a warmed serving dish.

Spoon the anchovy sauce into the dish and toss with the pasta, using 2 large forks. Garnish with the chopped parsley and serve immediately.

SERVES 2

5 oz/140 g dried macaroni
1 tbsp olive oil
1 garlic clove, crushed
2 oz/55 g white mushrooms, sliced
½ red bell pepper, thinly sliced

7 oz/200 g canned tuna in spring water, drained and flaked
½ tsp dried oregano
2 tbsp butter or margarine, plus extra for greasing
1 tbsp all-purpose flour

1 cup milk
2 tomatoes, sliced
2 tbsp dried breadcrumbs
½ cup shredded sharp cheddar or grated Parmesan cheese
salt and pepper

Tuna & Noodle Casserole

Preheat the oven to 400°F/200°C. Bring a large pan of lightly salted water to a boil. Add the pasta, bring back to a boil, and cook for 8–10 minutes, or until tender but still firm to the bite. Drain, rinse, and drain again thoroughly.

Heat the olive oil in a skillet and cook the garlic, mushrooms, and bell pepper until soft. Add the tuna and oregano and season to taste with salt and pepper. Heat through.

Grease a 4-cup/1-liter ovenproof dish with a little butter. Add half of the cooked macaroni, cover with the tuna mixture, then add the remaining macaroni.

Melt the butter in a pan, stir in the flour, and cook for 1 minute. Add the milk gradually and bring to a boil. Simmer for 1–2 minutes, stirring constantly, until thickened. Season to taste with salt and pepper. Pour the sauce over the macaroni. Lay the sliced tomatoes over the sauce and sprinkle with the breadcrumbs and cheese. Cook in the preheated oven for 25 minutes, or until piping hot and the top is well browned.

SERVES 4

7 oz/200 g dried egg ribbon pasta, such as tagliatelle
2 tbsp butter
2 oz/55 g fine fresh breadcrumbs
1¾ cups condensed canned cream of mushroom soup

4 fl oz/125 ml milk
2 celery stalks, chopped
1 red and 1 green bell pepper, cored, seeded, and chopped
5 oz/140 g sharp coarsely shredded cheddar cheese

2 tbsp chopped fresh parsley
7 oz/200 g canned tuna in oil, drained and flaked
salt and pepper

Cheesy Pasta Tuna Surprise

Preheat the oven to 400°F/200°C. Bring a large pan of salted water to a boil. Add the pasta and cook for 2 minutes less than specified on the package instructions.

Meanwhile, melt the butter in a separate, small pan over medium heat. Stir in the breadcrumbs, then remove from the heat and set aside.

Drain the pasta well and set aside. Pour the soup into the pasta pan over medium heat, then stir in the milk, celery, bell peppers, half the cheese, and the parsley. Add the tuna and gently stir in so that the flakes don't break up. Season to taste with salt and pepper. Heat just until small bubbles appear around the edge of the mixture, but do not boil. Stir the pasta into the pan and use 2 forks to mix all the ingredients together. Spoon the mixture into an ovenproof dish that is also suitable for serving and spread out.

Stir the remaining cheese into the buttered breadcrumbs, then sprinkle over the top of the pasta mixture. Bake in the oven for 20–25 minutes, until the topping is golden. Let stand for 5 minutes before serving straight from the dish.

SERVES 4

butter, for greasing
1 lb/450 g dried rigatoni
 (pasta tubes)
7 oz/200 g canned
 flaked tuna, drained

1 cup ricotta cheese
½ cup heavy cream
2 cups freshly grated
 Parmesan cheese

4 oz/115 g sun-dried
 tomatoes, drained and
 sliced
salt and pepper

Baked Tuna & Ricotta Rigatoni

Preheat the oven to 400°F/200°C. Lightly grease a large ovenproof dish with butter. Bring a large, heavy-bottom pan of lightly salted water to a boil. Add the rigatoni, return to a boil, and cook for 8–10 minutes, or until tender but still firm to the bite. Drain the pasta and let stand until cool enough to handle.

Meanwhile, mix the tuna and ricotta cheese together in a bowl to form a soft paste. Spoon the mixture into a pastry bag and use to fill the rigatoni. Arrange the filled pasta tubes side by side in the prepared dish.

To make the sauce, mix the cream and Parmesan cheese together in a bowl and season to taste with salt and pepper. Spoon the sauce over the rigatoni and top with the sun-dried tomatoes. Bake in the preheated oven for 20 minutes and then serve immediately.

SERVES 4

1 lb 2 oz/500 g dried
  spaghetti
2 tbsp butter
7 oz/200 g canned tuna,
  drained

2 oz/55 g canned
  anchovies, drained
1 cup olive oil
1 cup coarsely chopped
  fresh flat-leaf parsley

2/3 cup sour cream or
  yogurt
salt and pepper

Spaghetti with Tuna & Parsley

Bring a large, heavy-bottom pan of lightly salted water to a boil. Add the pasta, return to a boil, and cook for 8–10 minutes, or until tender but still firm to the bite. Drain the pasta and return to the pan. Add the butter, toss thoroughly to coat, and keep warm until needed.

Flake the tuna into smaller pieces using 2 forks. Place the tuna in a food processor or blender with the anchovies, olive oil, and parsley and process until the sauce is smooth. Pour in the sour cream and process for a few seconds to blend. Taste the sauce and season with salt and pepper, if necessary.

Shake the pan of spaghetti over medium heat for a few minutes, or until it is thoroughly warmed through.

Pour the sauce over the spaghetti and toss quickly, using 2 forks. Serve immediately.

SERVES 6

1 tbsp butter
8 oz/225 g shrimp, shelled, deveined, and coarsely chopped
1 lb/450 g monkfish fillets, skinned and chopped
8 oz/225 g cremini mushrooms, chopped

3½ cups store-bought béchamel sauce
14 oz/400 g canned chopped tomatoes
1 tbsp chopped fresh chervil
1 tbsp shredded fresh basil

8 lasagna sheets, cooked
¾ cup freshly grated Parmesan cheese
salt and pepper

Lasagna Alla Marinara

Preheat the oven to 375°F/190°C. Melt the butter in a large, heavy-bottom pan. Add the shrimp and monkfish and cook over medium heat for 3–5 minutes, or until the shrimp change color. Using a slotted spoon, transfer the shrimp to a small heatproof bowl. Add the mushrooms to the pan and cook, stirring occasionally, for 5 minutes. Transfer the fish and mushrooms to the bowl.

Stir the fish mixture, with any juices, into the béchamel sauce and season to taste with salt and pepper. Layer the tomatoes, chervil, basil, fish mixture, and lasagna sheets in a large ovenproof dish, ending with a layer of the fish mixture. Sprinkle evenly with the grated Parmesan cheese.

Bake in the preheated oven for 35 minutes, or until golden brown, then serve immediately.

SERVES 4

3 lb 5 oz/1.5 kg freshly cooked crabmeat, shells reserved
2 tbsp virgin olive oil
2 fresh red chiles, seeded and finely chopped
4 garlic cloves, finely chopped
1 lb 12 oz/800 g canned tomatoes

8 fl oz/225 ml dry white wine
12 oz/350 g dried spaghetti
2 tbsp butter
4 oz/115 g prepared squid, sliced
6 oz/175 g large shrimp

1 lb/450 g mussels, cleaned
3 tbsp coarsely chopped fresh flat-leaf parsley
1 tbsp shredded fresh basil leaves, plus extra sprigs to garnish
salt and pepper

Seafood Pasta Parcels

Carefully break up the larger pieces of crab shell with a meat mallet or the end of a rolling pin. Heat 1 tablespoon of the olive oil in a large saucepan. Add half the chiles and half the garlic, then add the pieces of crab shell. Cook over medium heat, stirring occasionally, for 2–3 minutes. Add the tomatoes with their can juices and the wine. Reduce the heat and simmer for about 1 hour. Strain the sauce, pressing down on the contents of the strainer with a wooden spoon. Season to taste with salt and pepper and set aside.

Preheat the oven to 350°F/180°C. Bring a large pan of lightly salted water to a boil. Add the pasta, bring back to a boil, and cook for 8–10 minutes, until tender but still firm to the bite. Drain and set aside. Heat the remaining oil with the butter in a large, heavy-bottom pan. Add the remaining chile and garlic, and cook over low heat, stirring occasionally, for 5 minutes, until soft. Add the squid, shrimp, and mussels, cover, and cook over high heat for 4–5 minutes, until the mussels have opened. Add the crabmeat and heat through for 2–3 minutes. Remove the pan from the heat and discard any mussels that remain closed. Add the pasta to the seafood with the chile-and-tomato sauce, parsley, and basil, tossing well to coat.

Cut out 4 large squares of parchment paper. Divide the pasta and seafood among them, placing it on one half. Fold over the other half and turn in the edges securely to seal. Transfer to a large baking sheet and bake in the preheated oven for about 10 minutes, until the parcels have puffed up. Serve immediately, garnished with the basil sprigs.

SERVES 4

6 tbsp butter, plus extra
  for greasing
12 oz/350 g dried
  macaroni
2 small fennel bulbs,
  thinly sliced

6 oz/175 g mushrooms,
  thinly sliced
6 oz/175 g cooked
  peeled shrimp
pinch of cayenne pepper
1¼ cups store-bought
  béchamel sauce

½ cup freshly grated
  Parmesan cheese
2 large tomatoes, halved
  and sliced
olive oil, for brushing
1 tsp dried oregano
salt

Shrimp & Pasta Casserole

Preheat the oven to 350°F/180°C. Grease a large ovenproof dish with butter. Bring a large pan of lightly salted water to a boil. Add the pasta, return to a boil, and cook for 8–10 minutes, or until tender but still firm to the bite. Drain and return to the pan. Add 2 tablespoons of the butter to the pasta, cover, shake the pan, and keep warm.

Melt the remaining butter in a separate pan. Add the fennel and cook for 3–4 minutes. Stir in the mushrooms and cook for an additional 2 minutes. Stir in the shrimp, then remove the pan from the heat.

Stir the cooked pasta, cayenne pepper, and the shrimp mixture into the béchamel sauce.

Pour the mixture into the prepared dish and spread evenly. Sprinkle the Parmesan cheese on top and arrange the tomato slices in a ring around the edge. Brush the tomatoes with olive oil, then sprinkle the oregano on top. Bake in the preheated oven for 25 minutes, or until golden brown. Serve immediately.

SERVES 4

8 oz/225 g dried penne
(pasta quills)
12 oz/350 g prepared
squid
6 tbsp olive oil
2 onions, sliced

1 cup fish stock or
chicken stock
2/3 cup full-bodied red
wine
14 oz/400 g canned
chopped tomatoes
2 tbsp tomato paste

1 tbsp chopped fresh
marjoram
1 bay leaf
salt and pepper
2 tbsp chopped fresh
flat-leaf parsley,
to garnish

Penne with Squid & Tomatoes

Bring a large, heavy-bottom pan of lightly salted water to a boil. Add the pasta, return to a boil, and cook for 3 minutes, then drain and set aside until ready to use. With a sharp knife, cut the squid into strips.

Heat the olive oil in a large saucepan. Add the onions and cook over low heat, stirring occasionally, for 5 minutes, or until softened. Add the squid and stock, bring to a boil, and simmer for 3 minutes. Stir in the wine, chopped tomatoes and their can juices, tomato paste, marjoram, and bay leaf. Season to taste with salt and pepper. Bring to a boil and cook for 5 minutes, or until slightly reduced.

Add the pasta, return to a boil, and simmer for 8–10 minutes, or until tender but still firm to the bite. Remove and discard the bay leaf. Transfer to a warmed serving dish, sprinkle with the parsley, and serve immediately.

SERVES 4

12 scallops
3 tbsp olive oil
12 oz/350 g dried
 conchiglie
 (pasta shells)

⅔ cup fish stock
1 onion, chopped
juice and finely grated
 rind of 2 lemons
½ cup heavy cream

2 cups shredded
 cheddar cheese
salt and pepper
crusty whole wheat
 bread, to serve

Baked Scallops with Pasta in Shells

Preheat the oven to 350°F/180°C. Remove the scallops from their shells. Scrape off the skirt and the black intestinal thread. Reserve the white part (the flesh) and the orange part (the coral or roe). Very carefully ease the flesh and coral from the shell with a short but very strong knife. Wash the shells thoroughly and dry them well. Put the shells on a cookie sheet. Sprinkle lightly with 2 tablespoons of the olive oil and set aside.

Meanwhile, bring a large pan of lightly salted water to a boil. Add the pasta and remaining olive oil and cook for about 8–10 minutes, or until tender but still firm to the bite. Drain and divide the pasta among the scallop shells.

Put the scallops, stock, and onion in an ovenproof dish and season to taste with pepper. Cover with foil and bake in the preheated oven for 8 minutes.

Remove the dish from the oven. Remove the foil and, using a slotted spoon, transfer the scallops to the shells. Add 1 tablespoon of the cooking liquid to each shell, together with a drizzle of lemon juice, a little lemon rind, and a little cream, then top with the shredded cheese.

Increase the oven temperature to 450°F/230°C and return the scallops to the oven for an additional 4 minutes. Serve the scallops in their shells with crusty whole wheat bread.

SERVES 6

1 lb/450 g shrimp
2 tbsp butter
2 shallots, finely chopped
1 cup dry white vermouth
1½ cups water

1 lb/450 g dried linguine
2 tbsp olive oil
1 lb/450 g prepared scallops, thawed if frozen

2 tbsp snipped fresh chives
salt and pepper

Linguine with Shrimp & Scallops

Shell and devein the shrimp, reserving the shells. Melt the butter in a heavy-bottom skillet. Add the shallots and cook over low heat, stirring occasionally, for 5 minutes, or until softened. Add the shrimp shells and cook, stirring constantly, for 1 minute. Pour in the vermouth and cook, stirring, for 1 minute. Add the water, bring to a boil, then reduce the heat and simmer for 10 minutes, or until the liquid has reduced by half. Remove the skillet from the heat.

Bring a large, heavy-bottom pan of lightly salted water to a boil. Add the pasta, return to a boil, and cook for 8–10 minutes, or until tender but still firm to the bite.

Meanwhile, heat the oil in a separate heavy-bottom skillet. Add the scallops and shrimp and cook, stirring frequently, for 2 minutes, or until the scallops are opaque and the shrimp have changed color. Strain the shrimp-shell stock into the skillet. Drain the pasta and add to the skillet with the chives and season to taste with salt and pepper. Toss well over low heat for 1 minute, then serve immediately.

SERVES 6

2 lb 12 oz/1.25 kg
   mussels, scrubbed and
   debearded
1 cup dry white wine
2 large onions, chopped

½ cup butter
6 large garlic cloves,
   finely chopped
5 tbsp chopped fresh
   parsley

1¼ cups heavy cream
14 oz/400 g dried
   conchiglie
   (pasta shells)
salt and pepper

Pasta Shells with Mussels

Discard any mussels with broken shells or any that refuse to close when tapped. Place the mussels in a large, heavy-bottom pan, together with the wine and half of the onions. Cover and cook over medium heat, shaking the pan frequently, for 2–3 minutes, or until the shells open. Remove the pan from the heat. Remove the mussels with a slotted spoon, reserving the cooking liquid. Discard any mussels that remain closed. Strain the cooking liquid through a cheesecloth-lined strainer into a bowl and set aside.

Melt the butter in a pan. Add the remaining onion and cook until translucent. Stir in the garlic and cook for 1 minute. Gradually stir in the reserved cooking liquid. Stir in the parsley and cream, and season to taste with salt and pepper. Bring to a simmer over low heat.

Meanwhile, bring a large pan of lightly salted water to a boil. Add the pasta and cook for 8–10 minutes, or until tender but still firm to the bite. Drain and keep warm.

Set aside a few mussels for the garnish and remove the remainder from their shells. Stir the shelled mussels into the cream sauce and warm briefly. Transfer the pasta to a serving dish. Pour the sauce on top and toss to coat. Garnish with the reserved mussels and serve.

SERVES 4

2 lb 4 oz/1 kg clams, scrubbed
1 cup dry white wine
2 garlic cloves, coarsely chopped

4 tbsp chopped fresh flat-leaf parsley
2 tbsp olive oil
1 onion, chopped
8 plum tomatoes, peeled, seeded, and chopped

1 fresh red chile, seeded and chopped
12 oz/350 g dried linguine
salt and pepper

Linguine with Clams in Tomato Sauce

Discard any clams with broken shells or any that refuse to close when tapped. Pour the wine into a large, heavy-bottom pan and add the garlic, half the parsley, and the clams. Cover and cook over high heat, shaking the pan occasionally, for 5 minutes, or until the shells have opened. Remove the clams with a slotted spoon, reserving the cooking liquid. Discard any that remain closed and remove half of the remainder from their shells. Keep the shelled and unshelled clams in separate covered bowls. Strain the cooking liquid through a cheesecloth-lined strainer and set aside.

Heat the olive oil in a heavy-bottom pan. Add the onion and cook over low heat for 5 minutes, or until softened. Add the tomatoes, chile, and reserved cooking liquid, and season to taste with salt and pepper. Bring to a boil, partially cover, and simmer for 20 minutes.

Meanwhile, bring a large, heavy-bottom pan of lightly salted water to a boil. Add the pasta, return to a boil, and cook for 8–10 minutes, or until tender but still firm to the bite. Drain and transfer to a warmed serving dish.

Stir the shelled clams into the tomato sauce and heat through gently for 2–3 minutes. Pour over the pasta and toss. Garnish with the clams in their shells and remaining parsley. Serve immediately.

SERVES 4

⅓ cup lemon pepper oil, plus extra for serving
6 cloves garlic, crushed
1½ lbs/675 g mixed seafood (shrimp, calamari, mussels)

dash of vodka
½ cup white wine
1 sprig tarragon, leaves only
dash of salt

1 lb/450 g dried fettuccine
flat-leaf parsley, chopped, to garnish

Fettuccine with Lemon Pepper Seafood

Heat a wok or deep skillet and add the lemon pepper oil. When the oil is hot, add the garlic and seafood. Stir for one minute. Add a dash of vodka, the white wine, tarragon leaves, and salt. Keep stirring until the seafood is cooked through.

Bring a pan of lightly salted water to a boil over medium heat. Add the pasta and cook for 8–10 minutes, or until tender but still firm to the bite. Drain and add the pasta to the seafood mixture. Toss well and serve immediately on warmed plates. Drizzle more lemon pepper oil on top to serve and garnish with the chopped flat-leaf parsley.

SERVES 4

6 scallions
12 oz/350 g crabmeat
2 tsp finely chopped fresh
  ginger
⅛–¼ tsp chili or Tabasco
  sauce

1 lb 9 oz/700 g tomatoes,
  peeled, seeded, and
  coarsely chopped
1 garlic clove, finely
  chopped
1 tbsp white wine vinegar
1 quantity Basic Pasta
  Dough (see p. 6)

all-purpose flour,
  for dusting
1 egg, lightly beaten
2 tbsp heavy cream
salt
shredded scallions,
  to garnish

Crab Ravioli

Thinly slice the scallions, keeping the white and green parts separate. Mix the scallion greens, crabmeat, ginger, and chili sauce to taste together in a bowl. Cover and chill.

Place the tomatoes in a food processor and process to a puree. Place the garlic, white parts of the scallions, and vinegar in a pan and add the pureed tomatoes. Bring to a boil, then reduce the heat and simmer for 10 minutes. Remove from the heat and set aside.

Divide the pasta in half and wrap 1 piece in plastic wrap. Roll out the other piece on a lightly floured counter to a rectangle ¹⁄₁₆–⅛ inch/2–3 mm thick. Cover with a damp dish towel and roll out the other piece of dough to the same size. Place small mounds, about 1 teaspoon each, of the crabmeat mixture in rows 1½ inches/ 4 cm apart on a sheet of pasta dough. Brush the spaces between the mounds with beaten egg. Lift the second sheet of dough on top of the first and press down firmly between the pockets of filling, pushing out any air bubbles. Using a pasta wheel or sharp knife, cut into squares. Place on a floured dish towel and let stand for 1 hour.

Bring a large pan of salted water to a boil. Add the ravioli and cook for 5 minutes. Remove with a slotted spoon and drain on paper towels. Gently heat the tomato sauce and whisk in the cream. Place the ravioli in serving dishes and pour the sauce on top. Serve, garnished with shredded scallions.

Vegetarian

SERVES 4

2½ cups milk
1 onion, peeled
8 peppercorns
1 bay leaf
4 tbsp butter
scant ⅓ cup all-purpose
    flour

½ tsp ground nutmeg
⅓ cup heavy cream
scant 1 cup shredded
    sharp cheddar cheese
3½ oz/100 g Roquefort
    cheese, crumbled

12 oz/350 g dried
    macaroni
scant 1 cup shredded
    Gruyère or Emmental
    cheese
pepper

Macaroni + Cheese

Put the milk, onion, peppercorns, and bay leaf in a pan and bring to a boil. Remove from the heat and let stand for 15 minutes.

Melt the butter in a pan and stir in the flour until well combined and smooth. Cook over medium heat, stirring constantly, for 1 minute. Remove from the heat. Strain the milk to remove the solids and stir a little into the butter-and-flour mixture until well incorporated. Return to the heat and gradually add the remaining milk, stirring constantly, until it has all been incorporated. Cook for an additional 3 minutes, or until the sauce is smooth and thickened, then add the nutmeg, cream, and season to taste with pepper. Add the cheddar and Roquefort cheeses and stir until melted.

Meanwhile, bring a large pan of water to a boil. Add the pasta, then return to a boil and cook for 8–10 minutes, or until just tender. Drain well and add to the cheese sauce. Stir well together.

Preheat the broiler to high. Spoon the mixture into an ovenproof serving dish, then scatter the Gruyère cheese on top and cook under the broiler until bubbling and brown. Serve immediately.

SERVES 4

3 tbsp olive oil
4 zucchini, halved lengthwise and thickly sliced
3 red bell peppers, seeded and chopped
1 eggplant, chopped
2 red onions, chopped

5 shallots, peeled and quartered
9 oz/250 g button mushrooms
14 oz/400 g canned chopped tomatoes
1 tbsp tomato paste
1¾ oz/50 g butter

1¾ oz/50 g plain flour
1 pint/600 ml milk
scant 1 cup cheddar cheese
8 lasagna sheets, cooked
2 tbsp grated Parmesan cheese
salt and pepper

Roasted Vegetable Lasagna

Preheat the oven to 375°F/190°C. Put the oil in a large bowl, add the zucchini, bell peppers, eggplant, onions, and shallots, and toss well to coat. Divide the vegetables between 2 baking sheets and roast in the preheated oven for 30–40 minutes, until soft and flecked with brown. Add the button mushrooms after 20 minutes. Remove the vegetables from the oven and turn into a large bowl. Add the tomatoes and tomato paste and mix well.

Melt the butter in a saucepan over a low heat. Stir in the flour and cook, stirring constantly, for 2–3 minutes. Gradually add the milk and cook, continuing to stir constantly, until the sauce is thick and smooth. Season to taste with salt and pepper and stir in the cheddar cheese.

Layer the vegetable mixture and sauce in an ovenproof dish with the lasagna, finishing with a layer of sauce. Sprinkle over the Parmesan cheese and bake in the oven for 30–35 minutes. Remove from the oven and serve hot.

SERVES 4

4 garlic cloves
4 cups pumpkin flesh
4 sun-dried tomatoes in
  oil, drained, plus 2 tbsp
  oil from the jar

½ cup ricotta cheese
1 tbsp finely chopped
  fresh rosemary
1 quantity Basic Pasta
  Dough (see p. 6)

all-purpose flour, for
  dusting
1 egg, lightly beaten
salt and pepper

Pumpkin & Ricotta Ravioli

Preheat the oven to 400°F/200°C. Place the unpeeled garlic cloves on a baking sheet and bake for 10 minutes. Meanwhile, put the pumpkin in a steamer set over a pan of boiling water. Cover and steam for 15 minutes, until tender.

Chop the sun-dried tomatoes. Squeeze the garlic cloves out of their skins into a bowl. Add the pumpkin, sun-dried tomatoes, ricotta, and rosemary and mash well with a potato masher until thoroughly combined. Season to taste with salt and pepper and let cool.

Divide the pasta dough in half and wrap 1 piece in plastic wrap. Roll out the other piece on a lightly floured surface to a rectangle $\frac{1}{16}$–$\frac{1}{8}$ inch/2–3 mm thick. Cover with a damp dish towel and roll out the other piece of dough to the same size. Place small mounds, about 1 teaspoon each, of the pumpkin filling in rows 1½ inches/4 cm apart on a sheet of pasta dough. Brush the spaces between the mounds with beaten egg. Lift the second sheet of dough on top and press down firmly between the pockets of filling, pushing out any air bubbles. Using a pasta wheel or sharp knife, cut into squares. Place on a floured dish towel and let stand for 1 hour.

Bring a large pan of salted water to a boil. Add the ravioli, bring back to a boil, and cook for 3–4 minutes, until tender. Drain, toss with the oil from the sun-dried tomatoes, and serve immediately.

SERVES 4

2 large eggplant
3 large zucchini
6 large tomatoes
1 large green bell pepper
1 large red bell pepper
3 garlic cloves
1 large onion

½ cup olive oil
2 tbsp tomato paste
½ tsp chopped fresh
    basil, plus extra sprigs
    to garnish
1 quantity Basic Pasta
    Dough (see p6)

all-purpose flour, for
    dusting
6 tbsp butter
⅔ cup light cream
¾ cup freshly grated
    Parmesan
salt and pepper

Vegetable Ravioli

To make the filling, cut the eggplant and zucchini into 1-inch/2.5-cm chunks.
Put the eggplant pieces into a strainer, sprinkle liberally with salt, and set aside for
20 minutes. Rinse and drain, then pat dry on paper towels.

Blanch the tomatoes in boiling water for 2 minutes. Drain, peel, and chop the flesh.
Core and seed the bell peppers and cut into 1-inch/2.5-cm dice. Chop the garlic
and onion. Heat the oil in a pan over low heat. Add the garlic and onion and cook
for about 3 minutes. Stir in the eggplant, zucchini, tomatoes, bell peppers, tomato
paste, and basil. Season to taste with salt and pepper, cover, and simmer for
20 minutes.

Roll out the pasta dough on a lightly floured counter to a rectangle ¹⁄₁₆–⅛ inch/
2–3 mm thick. Using a 2-inch/5-cm plain cookie cutter, stamp out rounds. Place
small mounds, about 1 teaspoon each, of the filling on half of the rounds. Brush the
edges with a little water, then cover with the remaining rounds, pressing the edges
to seal. Place on a floured dish towel and let stand for 1 hour. Preheat the oven to
400°F/200°C.

Bring a pan of lightly salted water to a boil over medium heat. Add the ravioli
and cook for about 3–4 minutes. Drain and transfer to an ovenproof dish, dotting
each layer with butter. Pour the cream on top then sprinkle the Parmesan cheese
over this. Cook in the preheated oven for 20 minutes. Garnish with basil and serve
immediately.

SERVES 4

1 lb/450 g dried
spaghetti
¾ cup (1½ sticks)
unsalted butter

4 tbsp chopped fresh
flat-leaf parsley

8 oz/225 g Parmesan
cheese, grated
salt

Spaghetti with Parsley & Parmesan

Bring a large pan of lightly salted water to a boil. Add the pasta, bring back to a boil, and cook for 8–10 minutes, or until tender but still firm to the bite. Drain and turn into a warmed serving dish.

Add the butter, parsley, and half the Parmesan cheese and toss well, using 2 forks, until the butter and cheese have melted. Divide among individual serving bowls and serve immediately sprinkled with the remaining Parmesan cheese.

SERVES 4

8 oz/225 g dried fusilli (pasta spirals)
1 head of broccoli, cut into florets
2 zucchini, sliced
8 oz/225 g asparagus spears, trimmed

2 cups snow peas
1 cup frozen peas
2 tbsp butter
3 tbsp vegetable stock
5 tbsp heavy cream
large pinch of freshly grated nutmeg

2 tbsp chopped fresh parsley
salt and pepper
2 tbsp freshly grated Parmesan cheese, to serve

Pasta with Green Vegetables

Bring a large, heavy-bottom pan of lightly salted water to a boil. Add the pasta, return to a boil, and cook for 8–10 minutes, or until tender but still firm to the bite. Drain well and return to the pan, cover, and keep warm.

Steam the broccoli, zucchini, asparagus spears, and snow peas over a pan of boiling, salted water until just starting to soften. Remove from the heat and plunge into cold water to prevent further cooking. Drain and reserve. Cook the peas in boiling, salted water for 3 minutes, then drain. Refresh in cold water and drain again.

Place the butter and vegetable stock in a pan over medium heat. Add all the vegetables, except for the asparagus spears, and toss carefully with a wooden spoon to heat through, being careful not to break them up. Stir in the cream, let the sauce heat through, and season to taste with salt, pepper, and nutmeg.

Transfer the pasta to a warmed serving dish and stir in the chopped parsley. Spoon the sauce over the pasta and arrange the asparagus spears on top. Serve hot with the freshly grated Parmesan.

SERVES 4

12 dried cannelloni tubes
1 eggplant
½ cup olive oil
1 cup fresh spinach
2 garlic cloves, crushed
1 tsp ground cumin
1¼ cups chopped
   mushrooms

2 oz/55 g mozzarella
   cheese, sliced
salt and pepper
corn salad, to garnish

tomato sauce
1 tbsp olive oil
1 onion, chopped

2 garlic cloves, crushed
1 lb 12 oz/800 g canned
   chopped tomatoes
1 tsp superfine sugar
2 tbsp chopped fresh
   basil

Vegetable Cannelloni

Preheat the oven to 375°F/190°C. Bring a large, heavy-bottom pan of lightly salted water to a boil. Add the cannelloni tubes, return to a boil, and cook for 8–10 minutes, or until tender but still firm to the bite. Transfer the pasta to a plate and pat dry with paper towels.

Cut the eggplant into small dice. Heat the oil in a skillet over medium heat. Add the eggplant and cook, stirring frequently, for about 2–3 minutes.

Add the spinach, garlic, cumin, and mushrooms and reduce the heat. Season to taste with salt and pepper and cook, stirring constantly, for 2–3 minutes. Spoon the mixture into the cannelloni tubes and arrange in a casserole in a single layer.

To make the sauce, heat the oil in a pan over medium heat. Add the onion and garlic and cook for 1 minute. Add the tomatoes, sugar, and basil and bring to a boil. Reduce the heat and simmer gently for about 5 minutes. Spoon the sauce over the cannelloni tubes.

Arrange the sliced mozzarella cheese on top of the sauce and cook in the preheated oven for about 30 minutes, or until the cheese is golden brown and bubbling. Serve immediately, garnished with corn salad.

SERVES 4

12 dried cannelloni tubes
6 tbsp olive oil, plus extra
  for brushing
1 onion, finely chopped
2 garlic cloves, finely
  chopped
1 lb 12 oz/800 g canned
  chopped tomatoes

1 tbsp tomato paste
8 black olives, pitted and
  chopped
2 tbsp butter
1 lb/450 g wild
  mushrooms, finely
  chopped
1½ cups fresh
  breadcrumbs

⅔ cup milk
1 cup ricotta cheese
6 tbsp freshly grated
  Parmesan cheese
2 tbsp pine nuts
2 tbsp slivered almonds
salt and pepper

Mushroom Cannelloni

Preheat the oven to 375°F/190°C. Bring a large pan of lightly salted water to a boil. Add the cannelloni tubes, return to a boil, and cook for 8–10 minutes, or until tender but still firm to the bite. With a slotted spoon, transfer the cannelloni tubes to a plate and pat dry. Brush a large ovenproof dish with olive oil.

Heat 2 tablespoons of the oil in a skillet, add the onion and half the garlic, and cook over low heat for 5 minutes, or until softened. Add the tomatoes and their can juices, tomato paste, and olives, and season to taste with salt and pepper. Bring to a boil and cook for 3–4 minutes. Pour the sauce into the ovenproof dish.

To make the filling, melt the butter in a heavy-bottom skillet. Add the mushrooms and remaining garlic and cook over medium heat, stirring frequently, for 3–5 minutes, or until tender. Remove the skillet from the heat. Mix the breadcrumbs, milk, and remaining oil together in a large bowl, then stir in the ricotta, mushroom mixture, and 4 tablespoons of the Parmesan cheese. Season to taste with salt and pepper.

Fill the cannelloni tubes with the mushroom mixture and place them in the dish. Brush with olive oil and sprinkle with the remaining Parmesan cheese, the pine nuts, and almonds. Bake in the oven for 25 minutes, or until golden. Serve immediately.

SERVES 4

1 lb/450 g dried
spaghetti
½ cup extra virgin olive oil

3 garlic cloves, finely
chopped
3 tbsp chopped fresh
flat-leaf parsley

salt and pepper

Spaghetti Olio E Aglio

Bring a large, heavy-bottom pan of lightly salted water to a boil. Add the pasta, return to a boil, and cook for 8–10 minutes, or until tender but still firm to the bite.

Meanwhile, heat the olive oil in a heavy-bottom skillet. Add the garlic and a pinch of salt and cook over low heat, stirring constantly, for 3–4 minutes, or until golden. Do not let the garlic brown or it will taste bitter. Remove the skillet from the heat.

Drain the pasta and transfer to a large, warmed serving dish. Pour in the garlic-flavored olive oil, then add the chopped parsley and season to taste with salt and pepper. Toss well and serve immediately.

SERVES 4

14 oz/400 g dried rigatoni (pasta tubes)
2 tbsp butter

6 fresh sage leaves
7 oz/200 g Gorgonzola cheese, diced

¾–1 cup heavy cream
2 tbsp dry vermouth
salt and pepper

Rigatoni with Gorgonzola Sauce

Bring a large, heavy-bottom pan of lightly salted water to a boil. Add the pasta, return to a boil, and cook for 8–10 minutes, until tender but still firm to the bite.

Meanwhile, melt the butter in a separate heavy-bottom pan. Add the sage leaves and cook, stirring gently, for 1 minute. Remove and set aside the sage leaves. Add the cheese and cook, stirring constantly, over low heat until it has melted. Gradually, stir in ¾ cup of the cream and the vermouth. Season to taste with salt and pepper and cook, stirring, until thickened. Add more cream if the sauce seems too thick.

Drain the pasta well and transfer to a warmed serving dish. Add the Gorgonzola sauce, toss well to mix, and serve immediately, garnished with the reserved sage leaves.

SERVES 4

1⅓ cups dried cannellini beans, soaked overnight
8 oz/225 g dried penne (pasta quills)
6 tbsp olive oil
3½ cups vegetable stock
2 large onions, sliced

2 garlic cloves, chopped
2 bay leaves
1 tsp dried oregano
1 tsp dried thyme
5 tbsp red wine
2 tbsp tomato paste
2 celery stalks, sliced
1 fennel bulb, sliced

4 oz/115 g mushrooms, sliced
8 oz/225 g tomatoes, sliced
1 tsp dark brown sugar
2 oz/55 g dry white breadcrumbs
salt and pepper
crusty bread, to serve

Pasta + Bean Casserole

Preheat the oven to 350°F/180°C. Drain the beans and put them in a large pan, then add water to cover and bring to a boil. Boil the beans rapidly for 20 minutes, then drain them and set aside.

Cook the pasta for 3 minutes in a large pan of boiling salted water, adding 1 tablespoon of the olive oil. Drain in a colander and set aside.

Put the beans in a large flameproof casserole, pour in the stock, and stir in the remaining olive oil, the onions, garlic, bay leaves, herbs, red wine, and tomato paste.

Bring to a boil, cover the casserole, and cook in the preheated oven for 2 hours.

Remove the casserole from the oven, add the reserved pasta, the celery, fennel, mushrooms, and tomatoes, and season to taste with salt and pepper. Stir in the sugar and sprinkle the breadcrumbs on top. Cover the casserole again, return to the oven, and continue cooking for 1 hour. Serve with crusty bread.

SERVES 4

6 tbsp butter, plus extra for greasing
5 oz/140 g fontina cheese, thinly sliced
1¼ cups store-bought béchamel sauce
12 oz/350 g mixed wild mushrooms, sliced
12 oz/350 g dried tagliatelle
2 egg yolks
4 tbsp freshly grated romano cheese
salt and pepper

Baked Pasta with Mushrooms

Preheat the oven to 400°F/200°C. Lightly grease a large ovenproof dish. Stir the fontina cheese into the béchamel sauce and set aside.

Melt 2 tablespoons of the butter in a large pan. Add the mushrooms and cook over low heat, stirring occasionally, for 10 minutes.

Meanwhile, bring a large pan of lightly salted water to a boil. Add the pasta, return to a boil, and cook for 8–10 minutes, or until tender but still firm to the bite. Drain, return to the pan, and add the remaining butter, the egg yolks, and about one-third of the sauce, then season with salt and pepper. Toss well to mix, then gently stir in the mushrooms.

Spoon the pasta mixture into the prepared dish. Pour the remaining sauce on top evenly and sprinkle with the grated romano cheese. Bake in the preheated oven for 15–20 minutes, or until golden brown, then serve immediately.

SERVES 4

10½ oz/300 g dried pasta of your choice
2 tbsp olive oil
9 oz/250 g white mushrooms, sliced

1 tsp dried oregano
scant 1¼ cups vegetable stock
1 tbsp lemon juice

6 tbsp cream cheese
1 cup frozen spinach leaves
salt and pepper

Creamy Spinach & Mushroom Pasta

Bring a large pan of lightly salted water to a boil. Add the pasta, bring back to a boil, and cook for 8–10 minutes, or until tender but still firm to the bite. Drain, reserving ¾ cup of the cooking liquid.

Meanwhile, heat the oil in a large, heavy-bottom skillet over medium heat, add the mushrooms, and cook, stirring frequently, for 8 minutes, or until almost crisp. Stir in the oregano, stock, and lemon juice and cook for 10–12 minutes, or until the sauce is reduced by half.

Stir in the cream cheese and spinach and cook over medium–low heat for 3–5 minutes. Add the reserved cooking liquid, then the cooked pasta. Stir well, season to taste with salt and pepper, and heat through before serving immediately.

SERVES 4

2 tbsp olive oil
2 yellow bell peppers,
  seeded and chopped
1 mild onion, finely
  chopped
1 small eggplant,
  chopped

14 oz/400 g canned
  chopped tomatoes
  with herbs
1 tbsp tomato paste
2 tbsp hot water, plus
  extra if needed
2¼ cups dried whole
  wheat pasta spirals

1 cup shredded cheddar
  cheese
generous ¾ cup slightly
  stale whole wheat or
  white breadcrumbs
salt and pepper

Cheesy Pasta Casserole

Heat the oil in a large, nonstick skillet over medium heat, then add the bell peppers, onion, and eggplant and cook, stirring occasionally, for 15 minutes, or until soft.

Add the tomatoes and their juices, tomato paste, hot water, salt, and pepper to taste to the skillet and stir well. Bring to a simmer and cook for 15 minutes. Stir in a little more water if the mixture is not fairly sloppy. Preheat the oven to 375°F/190°C.

Bring a pan of lightly salted water to a boil over medium heat. Add the pasta and cook for 8-10 minutes, or until tender but still firm to the bite. Drain and turn into a shallow ovenproof dish. Add the tomato mixture and mix together well. Spread out evenly in the dish.

Mix the cheddar cheese and breadcrumbs together, then sprinkle evenly over the pasta mixture. Bake in the preheated oven for 20-25 minutes, or until the top is golden. Serve immediately.

SERVES 4

2 tbsp olive oil
1 tbsp butter
1 small onion, finely chopped
4 bell peppers, yellow and red, seeded and cut into ¾-inch/2-cm squares

3 garlic cloves, thinly sliced
1 lb/450 g dried rigatoni (pasta tubes)
4½ oz/125 g goat cheese, crumbled

15 fresh basil leaves, shredded
10 black olives, pitted and sliced
salt and pepper

Rigatoni with Bell Peppers + Goat Cheese

Heat the oil and butter in a large skillet over medium heat. Add the onion and cook until soft. Raise the heat to medium–high and add the bell peppers and garlic. Cook for 12–15 minutes, stirring, until the peppers are tender but not mushy. Season to taste with salt and pepper. Remove from the heat.

Bring a large saucepan of lightly salted water to a boil. Add the pasta, bring back to a boil, and cook for 8–10 minutes, or until tender but still firm to the bite. Drain and transfer to a warmed serving dish. Add the goat cheese and toss to mix.

Briefly reheat the onion-and-pepper mixture. Add the basil and olives. Pour over the pasta and toss well to mix. Serve immediately.

SERVES 2–4

12 oz/350 g fresh pasta shapes
salt
6 tbsp olive oil

½ tsp freshly grated nutmeg
½ tsp black pepper
1 garlic clove, crushed
2 tbsp tapenade

½ cup black or green olives, pitted and sliced
1 tbsp chopped fresh parsley, to garnish (optional)

Pasta with Spicy Olive Sauce

Bring a large pan of lightly salted water to a boil. Add the pasta and cook for 8–10 minutes, or until tender but firm to the bite.

Meanwhile, put ½ teaspoon of salt with the oil, nutmeg, pepper, garlic, tapenade, and olives in another saucepan and heat slowly but do not let boil. Cover and let stand for 3 to 4 minutes.

Drain the pasta and return to the pan. Add the flavored oil and heat gently for 1 to 2 minutes. Serve immediately, garnished with chopped parsley, if using.

SERVES 4

12 oz/350 g dried vermicelli
3 zucchini
3 carrots
2 tbsp butter
1 tbsp olive oil

2 garlic cloves, finely chopped
½ cup fresh basil, shredded
2 tbsp snipped fresh chives

2 tbsp chopped fresh flat-leaf parsley
1 small head of radicchio, leaves shredded
salt and pepper

Vermicelli with Vegetable Ribbons

Bring a large, heavy-bottom pan of lightly salted water to a boil. Add the pasta, return to a boil, and cook for 8–10 minutes, or until tender but still firm to the bite.

Meanwhile, cut the zucchini and carrots into very thin strips with a swivel-blade vegetable peeler or a mandoline. Melt the butter with the olive oil in a heavy-bottom skillet. Add the carrot strips and garlic and cook over low heat, stirring occasionally, for 5 minutes. Add the zucchini strips and all the herbs and season to taste with salt and pepper.

Drain the pasta and add it to the skillet. Toss well to mix and cook, stirring occasionally, for 5 minutes. Transfer to a warmed serving dish, add the radicchio, toss well, and serve immediately.

SERVES 4

6 tbsp olive oil
1 small onion, very thinly sliced
2 garlic cloves, very finely chopped
2 tbsp chopped fresh rosemary

1 tbsp chopped fresh flat-leaf parsley
4 small zucchini, about 1 lb/450 g, cut into 1½-inch/4-cm lengths
finely grated rind of 1 lemon

1 lb/450 g dried fusilli (pasta spirals)
salt and pepper
freshly grated Parmesan cheese, to serve

Fusilli with Zucchini & Lemon

Heat the oil in a large skillet over medium–low heat. Add the onion and cook gently, stirring occasionally, for about 10 minutes, or until golden.

Raise the heat to medium–high. Add the garlic, rosemary, and parsley. Cook for a few seconds, stirring.

Add the zucchini and lemon rind. Cook for 5–7 minutes, stirring occasionally, until the zucchini are just tender. Season to taste with salt and pepper. Remove from the heat.

Bring a large saucepan of lightly salted water to a boil. Add the pasta, bring back to a boil, and cook for 8–10 minutes, or until tender but still firm to the bite. Drain and transfer to a warmed serving dish.

Briefly reheat the zucchini sauce. Pour over the pasta and toss well to mix. Sprinkle with the Parmesan cheese and serve immediately.

SERVES 4

⅓ cup olive oil
1 onion, finely chopped
1 cup black olives, pitted
    and coarsely chopped

14 oz/400 g canned
    chopped tomatoes,
    drained
2 red, yellow, or orange
    bell peppers, seeded
    and cut into thin strips

12 oz/350 g dried
    fettuccine
salt and pepper
shavings of Romano
cheese, to serve

Fettuccine with Bell Peppers + Olives

Heat the oil in a large, heavy-bottom pan. Add the onion and cook over low heat, stirring occasionally, for 5 minutes, or until softened. Add the olives, tomatoes, and bell peppers, and season to taste with salt and pepper. Cover and let simmer gently over very low heat, stirring occasionally, for 35 minutes.

Meanwhile, bring a large, heavy-bottom pan of lightly salted water to a boil. Add the pasta, return to a boil, and cook for 8–10 minutes, or until tender but still firm to the bite. Drain the pasta and transfer to a warmed serving dish.

Spoon the sauce onto the pasta and toss well. Sprinkle generously with the Romano cheese and serve immediately.

SERVES 4

2 garlic cloves
¾ cup hazelnuts
1 cup arugula, coarse
 stalks removed

1⅓ cups freshly grated
 Parmesan cheese, plus
 extra to serve
6 tbsp extra virgin olive oil

½ cup mascarpone
 cheese
14 oz/400 g dried
 spaghetti
salt and pepper

Spaghetti with Arugula & Hazelnut Pesto

Put the garlic and hazelnuts in a food processor and process until finely chopped. Add the arugula, Parmesan, and olive oil and process until smooth and thoroughly combined. Scrape the pesto into a serving dish, season to taste with salt and pepper, and stir in the mascarpone.

Bring a large pan of lightly salted water to a boil. Add the pasta, bring back to a boil, and cook for 8–10 minutes, until tender but still firm to the bite.

Stir ½–⅔ cup of the pasta cooking water into the pesto, mixing well until thoroughly combined. Drain the pasta, add it to the bowl, and toss well to coat. Sprinkle with extra Parmesan and serve immediately.

SERVES 4

1 onion, chopped
14 oz/400 g canned
    chopped tomatoes
1 cup milk

1–2 red chiles, seeded
    and finely chopped
1 garlic clove, finely
    chopped
pinch of ground
    coriander

10 oz/280 g dried
    conchiglie
    (pasta shells)
¾ cup shredded Gruyère
    cheese
salt and pepper

Hot Tomato & Pasta Shell Gratin

Put the onion, tomatoes, and milk in a large, heavy-bottom pan and bring just to a boil. Add the chiles, garlic, coriander, and pasta, season to taste with salt and pepper, and cook over medium heat, stirring frequently, for 2–3 minutes.

Add just enough water to cover and cook, stirring frequently, for 8–10 minutes, until the pasta is tender but still firm to the bite. Meanwhile, preheat the broiler.

Spoon the pasta mixture into individual flameproof dishes and sprinkle evenly with the cheese. Place under the broiler for 3–4 minutes, until the cheese has melted. Serve immediately.

SERVES 4

1 red bell pepper
1 orange bell pepper
10 oz/280 g dried
   conchiglie
   (pasta shells)

5 tbsp extra virgin olive oil
2 tbsp lemon juice
2 tbsp pesto
1 garlic clove, very finely
   chopped

3 tbsp shredded fresh
   basil leaves
salt and pepper

Pasta Salad with Bell Peppers

Put the whole bell peppers on a baking sheet and place under a preheated broiler, turning frequently, for 15 minutes, until charred all over. Remove with tongs and place in a bowl. Cover with crumpled paper towels and set aside.

Meanwhile, bring a large pan of lightly salted water to a boil. Add the pasta, bring back to a boil, and cook for 8–10 minutes, until tender but still firm to the bite.

Combine the olive oil, lemon juice, pesto, and garlic in a bowl, whisking well to mix. Drain the pasta, add it to the pesto mixture while still hot, and toss well. Set aside.

When the bell peppers are cool enough to handle, peel off the skins, then cut open and remove the seeds. Chop the flesh coarsely and add to the pasta with the basil. Season to taste with salt and pepper and toss well. Serve at room temperature.

SERVES 4

butter for greasing
9 oz/250 g fusilli
1 lb/450 g purple
 sprouting broccoli
6 tbsp olive oil, plus extra
 for drizzling

2 shallots, thinly sliced
1 fresh red chile, seeded
 and finely chopped
2 garlic cloves, finely
 chopped

1 cup coarse fresh
 breadcrumbs
 (from a ciabatta loaf)
1 cup coarsely grated
 Parmesan cheese
salt and pepper

Pasta & Broccoli Gratin

Preheat the oven to 400°F/200°C. Butter a deep 2½-quart/2.5-liter ovenproof dish. Bring a pan of lightly salted water to the boil over medium heat. Add the pasta and cook for 8–10 minutes, or until tender but still firm to the bite. Drain thoroughly and turn into the ovenproof dish.

Meanwhile, cut up the sprouting broccoli and put the florets, leaves, and stems in a steamer basket set over boiling water. Steam for 4 minutes, until only just tender. Remove from the heat and set aside, reserving the water in the pan.

Heat a skillet over medium–low heat. Add the oil and gently cook the shallots, chile, and garlic for 5 minutes until softened and just starting to color.

Add the broccoli and ⅔ cup of the broccoli cooking water to the pasta in the ovenproof dish. Season with salt and pepper, and toss to mix. Add the shallot mixture and the oil from the skillet. Toss again to mix.

Scatter the breadcrumbs over the top, then sprinkle with the Parmesan and a little more salt and pepper. Drizzle the crumbs with more oil. Bake in the oven for 15–20 minutes, until golden and crisp.

SERVES 4

4 plum tomatoes, peeled, seeded, and chopped
4 garlic cloves, finely chopped
8 black olives, pitted and finely chopped

1 red chile, seeded and finely chopped
2 tbsp chopped fresh flat-leaf parsley
2 tbsp extra virgin olive oil

1 tbsp lemon juice
10 oz/280 g dried fettuccine
salt and pepper

Fettuccine with Garlic, Tomatoes + Olives

Place the tomatoes in a large, nonmetallic strainer set over a bowl. Cover and set aside in the refrigerator for 30 minutes.

Combine the garlic, olives, chile, parsley, oil, and lemon juice in a separate bowl. Season to taste with salt and pepper. Cover and set aside in the refrigerator until required. Add the tomatoes to the garlic mixture, discarding the drained juice.

Bring a large pan of lightly salted water to a boil. Add the fettuccine, return to a boil, and cook for 8–10 minutes, or until tender but still firm to the bite. Drain, then turn into a warmed serving bowl. Add the garlic and tomato mixture and toss well. Serve immediately.

SERVES 4-6

4 tbsp butter, plus extra for greasing
2 eggplant, sliced crosswise into ¾-inch/ 2-cm slices
olive oil for brushing
1 onion, chopped
2 large garlic cloves, finely chopped
½ tsp dried oregano
2 small strips lemon peel
1 lb 5 oz/600 g canned chopped tomatoes
10 oz/280 g penne
1 egg, lightly beaten
2½ cups coarsely shredded mozzarella cheese
½ cup Parmesan cheese shavings
salt and pepper

Penne with Mozzarella, Broiled Eggplant & Tomato Sauce

Preheat the oven to 400°F/200°C. Butter a deep 2½-quart/2.5-liter ovenproof dish. Arrange the eggplant in a single layer on a broiler pan. Brush with olive oil on both sides, and place under a very hot broiler. Broil for 10–12 minutes, turning once, until lightly colored. Transfer to a plate, season with salt and pepper, and keep warm.

Heat the butter in a skillet over medium heat. Add the onion and gently cook for 7 minutes, until starting to color. Add the garlic, oregano, and lemon peel and cook for another minute. Stir in the tomatoes and season to taste with salt and pepper. Bring to a boil, then reduce the heat and simmer for 5–7 minutes, until slightly reduced.

Meanwhile, bring a large pan of lightly salted water to a boil. Add the pasta and cook for 8–10 minutes, or until tender but still firm to the bite. Drain, return to the pan, and stir in the beaten egg.

Butter a high-sided 4½-pint/2.5-liter gratin dish. Turn half the penne into the bottom of the prepared dish. Arrange the eggplant slices in a single layer on top, and sprinkle with half the mozzarella cheese. Pour the tomato sauce over the eggplant, followed by the remaining penne. Sprinkle with the remaining mozzarella cheese and scatter the Parmesan shavings over the top. Bake in the oven for 20 minutes, until the top is golden and crisp.